MW01268401

Edmond Tyllney: Master of the Revels and Censor of Plays

AMS Studies in the Renaissance: No. 15
ISSN: 0195-657X

Other Titles in This Series:

1. Hilton Landry, ed. *New Essays on Shakespeare's Sonnets.* 1976.
2. J. W. Williamson. *The Myth of the Conqueror: Prince Henry Stuart, a Study in 17th Century Personation.* 1978.
3. Philip C. McGuire and David A. Samuelson, eds. *Shakespeare: The Theatrical Dimension.* 1979.
4. Paul Ramsey. *The Fickle Glass: A Study of Shakespeare's Sonnets.* 1979.
5. n.p.
6. Raymond C. Shady and G. B. Shand, eds. *Play-Texts in Old Spelling: Papers from the Glendon Conference.* 1984.
7. Mark Taylor. *Shakespeare's Darker Purpose: A Question of Incest.* 1982.
8. Kenneth Friedenreich, ed. *"Accompaninge the players": Essays Celebrating Thomas Middleton, 1581-1980.* 1983.
9. Sarah P. Sutherland. *Masques in Jacobean Tragedy.* 1982.
10. Margaret Loftus Ranald. *Shakespeare and His Social Context:* 1986.
11. Anne Lancashire, ed., Clifford Leech. *Christopher Marlowe: Poet for the Stage.* 1986.
12. C. J. Gianakaris, et al., eds. *Drama in the Renaissance.* 1986.
13. Georgianna Ziegler, ed. *Shakespeare Study Today.* 1986.
14. Kenneth Friedenreich, et al., eds. *"A Poet and a filthy Playmaker." New Essays on Christopher Marlowe.* 1986.

EDMOND TYLLNEY

Master of the Revels
and
Censor of Plays:
A Descriptive Index
to His
Diplomatic Manual on Europe

W. R. STREITBERGER

AMS PRESS, INC.
NEW YORK

Library of Congress Cataloging-in-Publication Data
Streitberger, W. R.
Edmond Tyllney, master of the revels and censor of plays.
(AMS studies in the Renaissance, ISSN 0195-657X; no. 15)
Bibliography: p.
1. Tilney, Edmund, d. 1610. Topographical descriptions, regiments, and policies of Italy, France, Germany, Netherlands, Spain, England, Scotland, and Ireland. 2. Europe—History—1517-1618—Sources. 3. Tilney, Edmund, d. 1610. I. Title. II. Series. D220.S77 1986 940.2'3 85-47998
ISBN 0-404-62285-2

Copyright © 1986 AMS Press Inc.
All rights reserved.
Manufactured in the USA

For Ona and Aaron

Contents

Preface

Edmond Tyllney [Tylney, Tilney, Tillney] (ca. 1536–1610), author of the "Topographical Descriptions, Regiments, and Policies of Italy, France, Germany [with Switzerland, Poland, Hungary, and Denmark], [the Netherlands], Spain [with Portugal], England [with Wales], Scotland, and Ireland [with Man, Wight, Jersey, and Guernsey]," (ca. 1603), was Master of the Revels at the English court from 1579 until his death. A talented administrator, Tyllney became censor of plays in 1581 and built the Revels Office into the powerful instrument by which the central government exercised its control over the drama. His primary task was to eliminate offensive discussion of political and religious issues on the stage which he accomplished by having all dramatic manuscripts submitted to his criticism for alteration or approval before they were publicly acted.

Tyllney himself had some reputation as an author. His *Flower of Friendship,* published in 1568 and dedicated to his distant cousin, Queen Elizabeth I, went through at least seven editions by 1587. But he was a courtier, primarily interested in his public career, and wrote only to further his ambition. The "Topographical Descriptions," a confidential, diplomatic reference work on the major countries of western Europe, intended as a manual for use in conducting foreign policy, appears to have been written in an attempt to secure a higher position for himself at court. His hopes for promotion, however, were not realized and his manuscript, prepared initially for Queen Elizabeth and, later, dedicated to King James I, seems never to have been actually presented. This work was one of the first attempts to compile indispensable intelligence information and to organize it into a highly structured and carefully indexed reference manual. The selection as well as the amount of information Tyllney included makes his work the most complete contemporary description of Europe in the age of Elizabeth extant in the language. It also contributes to our information about Tyllney's qualifications to censor political material in the drama. For here we have in over a quarter of a million words the political life's work of the man whose job it was to see that the politics of dramatists such as Marlowe, Shakespeare, and Jonson were innocuous enough for public consumption.

A full edition of the "Topographical Descriptions" would occupy over a thousand pages of typescript. Publishing such an edition would not only be prohibitively expensive but also would not serve the best interest of scholars. Various aspects of the work will be of interest to researchers in a variety of fields—social and diplomatic history, history of dramatic censorship, cartography, engraving, heraldry, genealogy, etc. But the work is so wide-ranging that much of the material would not be of sufficient interest to any one of them. A selected edition represents an unhappy compromise for similar reasons. Interested scholars will want to consult the work themselves, but since it exists in two distinct states (Folger MS., ca. 1600–1; Illinois MS., ca. 1603), each containing material not found in the other, the task would prove difficult at best. Consequently I have settled on a descriptive index, designed to help scholars assess the significance of the work and to facilitate study of it. In the chapters included the "Topographical Descriptions" is discussed in terms of its relation to Tyllney's career as Master of the Revels and censor of plays, in terms of its historical and literary significance, its sources and influences, stages of revision, and provenance. A full description of both states of the manuscript and a descriptive index to their contents are also provided.

The staffs of the University of Illinois Library, the Folger Library, the Huntington Library, Newberry Library, Surrey Archives, Greater London Record Office, Public Record Office, British Library, and Bodleian Library have all been particularly generous with their help on this project, as were the librarians at Yale, Harvard, Grolier Club, Suffolk Record Office, the Royal Commission on Historical Manuscripts, the American Antiquarian Society, and the booksellers, Stonehill, Dawsons, Quaritch, and Breslauer, who checked records or examined copies of rare books for me. Professors Allan Holaday, Mark Eccles, T. W. Baldwin, B. A. Milligan, J. Stillinger, F. J. Levy, Lloyd Berry, C. Koeman, A. N. L. Munby, Sir Anthony Wagner, Maj. J. More-Molyneux, and Laetitia Yeandle have provided invaluable advice and help with the project. I am grateful to the Folger Library, the Huntington Library, and the NEH for grants which enabled me to spend several summers carrying on research for various aspects of the project. The University of Washington Graduate School has generously provided a subvention to help publish this work.

Seattle, 1985

Abbreviations

B.M. *Maps* *British Museum Catalogue of Printed Maps, Charts, and Plans* (London, 1967). 15 vols.

Chambers, *Eliz. Stage* E. K. Chambers, *The Elizabethan Stage* (Oxford: Clarendon Press, 1923). 4 vols.

C.S.P. Dom. *Calendar of State Papers, Domestic Series, of the Reigns of Edward VI, Mary, and Elizabeth I,* ed. M. A. E. Green (London, 1856–72). 12 vols.

Complete Peerage G. E. Cokayne, *The Complete Peerage of England, Scotland, Ireland, Great Britain, and the United Kingdom, Extant, Extinct, or Dormant,* rev. ed., Vicary Gibbs et al. (London: St. Catherine's Press, 1910–59). 13 vols. in 14.

De Ricci Seymour De Ricci and W. J. Wilson, *Census of Medieval and Renaissance Manuscripts in the United States and Canada* (New York: H. W. Wilson Co., 1935–40). 3 vols.

Eccles, *Buc* Mark Eccles, "Sir George Buc, Master of the Revels," in *Thomas Lodge and Other Elizabethans,* ed. C. J. Sisson (Cambridge, Mass.: Harvard University Press, 1933).

Feuillerat, *Documents* Albert Feuillerat, *Documents Relating to the Office of the Revels in the time of Queen Elizabeth,* in *Materialen zur Kunde des älteren englischen Dramas,* ed. W. Bang (Louvain, 1908), vol. 21.

Heawood E. A. Heawood, *Watermarks,* in *Monumenta Chartae Papyracae,* ed. E. J. Labarre (Hilversum: Paper Pub. Co., 1950), vol. 1.

Hind A. M. Hind, *Engraving in England in the Sixteenth and Seventeenth Centuries: A Descriptive Catalogue* (Cambridge, 1952–64). 3 vols.

Hollstein F. W. R. Hollstein, *Dutch and Flemish Etchings, Engravings, and Woodcuts, c. 1450–1700* (Amsterdam: Hertzberger, 1949–76). 19 vols.

Koeman C. Koeman, *Atlantes Neerlandici* (Amsterdam: Theatrum Orbis Terrarum, 1967–71). 5 vols.

Manning and Bray Owen Manning and William Bray, *The History and Antiquities of Surrey* (London: J. Nichols, 1804–14). 3 vols.

Skelton R. A. Skelton, *County Atlases of the British Isles, 1579–1850* (London: Carta Press, 1970).

Shirley R. W. Shirley, "Early Printed Maps of the British Isles, 1477–1650," *Map Collector's Circle,* no. 95 (1974).

Streitberger, *Maps* W. R. Streitberger, "Five Rare Maps: Peter Overadt's 'Italy,' 'France,' 'Germany,' and 'Spain' (1598); and Peter van den Keere's 'England' (ca. 1600)," *Imago Mundi,* 17 (1975), 47–51.

I
Edmond Tyllney

I

EDMOND TYLLNEY, author of the "Topographical Descriptions, Regiments, and Policies of Italy, France, Germany, Netherlands, Spain, England, Scotland, and Ireland," was born, probably in 1536,[1] to Phillip Tyllney, Usher of the Privy Chamber to Henry VIII, and Malyn Chambre, Chamberwoman to Queen Catherine Howard. His family could be traced back to Frodo, who held a number of lordships in East Anglia under William the Conqueror, and hence was one of the most ancient families of knight's degree in England.[2] His grandfather, Sir Phillip, was Treasurer in the Scottish Wars under Thomas Howard, Earl of Surrey, later the second Duke of Norfolk. This Duke first married Sir Phillip's cousin, Elizabeth; after her death, he married Sir Phillip's sister, Agnes. The issue of these two marriages provided England with three Queens—Anne Boleyn, Catherine Howard, and Elizabeth I—and allied the Tyllneys by blood or marriage with virtually every important family in sixteenth-century England.[3]

Edmond's early life was spent in the shadow of disgrace. His mother, involved in the scandal surrounding the Queen's adultery, along with the Dowager Duchess of

Norfolk, Lord William, and other members of the Howard household, was convicted of misprision of treason for knowing of Catherine's "carnal, voluptuous, and licentious life" and "traitorously" concealing it from the king.[4] She was sentenced to life imprisonment and loss of goods in February 1543, but was pardoned after the principals in the case were executed. Edmond's father died in debt in 1541, and the boy was thus left in the care of his mother at a very difficult time in her life. They were probably taken into the household of the Dowager Duchess, Agnes (Tyllney) Howard, for the records of the Tyllney family which have survived indicate a close connection with the Howards throughout the century.[5] If Edmond was brought up under Howard supervision, this may explain why there is no record of his enrollment either at a leading university or at one of the Inns of Court. The Howards were not known in the sixteenth century for their formal educations but rather for their brilliant military and political service to the Tudors and the practical experience such service provided.[6]

What kind of an education was provided for him can only be surmised from his later career. He was roughly the same age as his cousin, Charles Howard, later Lord Admiral and Earl of Nottingham, and, while they do not seem to have been educated together, both direct and circumstantial evidence suggests that Edmond was provided with the necessary experience that might earn him a minor position at court. This would have included instruction in Latin as well as some modern foreign languages, history, government, travel on the Continent, and military and political experience. The sources that he later employed for his "Topographical Descriptions" indicate a firm grounding in Latin and at least a reading knowledge of Spanish, French, and Italian. The esteem in which Edmond was held by the Howard family is indicated by his position as chief mourner at the funeral of Edward, Lord William's third son, in April 1569.[7] That esteem is evident in other ways also. For Edmond's practical education seems to have been integrated with the Howards' own attempt to extend their influence in Surrey and at the court beginning in the 1550s and 1560s. Charles Howard had been elected to the House of Commons in 1562, and when he was returned to Parliament in 1572, Tyllney was then elected as a Burgess for Gatton, a position that his successor in the Revels Office, Sir George Buc, also a dependent of the Howards, was later to hold.[8] Stowe mentions a "master Tilney" who went in 1573 to the siege of Edinburgh castle, but while military experience would have been one of the important aspects of his early practical education, it is not clear that this was Edmond.[9] Charles Howard received two important commissions, one as General of the Horse under the Earl of Warwick in 1569–70 and one in the summer of 1571 to cruise the Channel to observe the Spanish fleet then assembling in the Netherlands to bring Phillip II's new bride, Anne of Austria, to Spain. There was, then, ample opportunity for Edmond to have gained military experience in the south. No direct evidence of his travel experience survives. But attitudes during the period toward the importance of travel as part of practical preparation for public service, the fact that the Howards provided Sir George Buc with travel opportunities, and Edmond's later mention as a possible envoy to Spain, suggest some foreign experience.

Tyllney's most important asset was his influence with a family that was to be intimately connected with the affairs of state and one that was a chief supporter of the developing drama during the Elizabethan period. Lord William, sympathetic to Elizabeth during Mary's reign, was rewarded for his loyalty with the post of Lord Chamberlain, a position he held from 1558 until 1572. It was the Lord Chamberlain rather than the Lord Great Chamberlain (hereditary in the house of Oxford) who was the chief officer at court, except on ceremonial occasions. His duties included regular attendance at court and his power was considerable, for he had charge of numerous departments in the Royal household, made arrangements for lodgings at court, presided over the banqueting hall, planned the entertainments, made arrangements for the summer progresses, received foreign ambassadors, and conducted those who were entitled into the presence of the Queen.[10] His constant association with the Queen, with influential members of the court, and with foreign ambassadors gave him a greater opportunity than even court favorites to suggest appointments to vacancies throughout the government. Since some of the offices over which he presided affected not only the Queen's comfort and pleasure, but also the court's prestige, the burden of choosing reliable candidates was a great one. From childhood Tyllney must have had an intimate familiarity with the Lord Chamberlain's duties, and this practical experience no doubt paved the way eventually for his appointment as Master of the Revels.

As part of his bid for recognition at court Tyllney published *A brief and pleasant discourse on the duties in marriage, called the Flower of Friendshippe* (1568) and dedicated it to his distant cousin, the Queen.[11] His talent as a writer was inspiring enough to prompt F. S. Boas to wonder if the cares of office prevented him from fulfilling in maturity "the literary promise of his younger years."[12] C. S. Lewis regarded the work as an attempt, albeit unsuccessful, to "create that world of courtesy which we find in Sidney's romance or in Lyly's or Shakespeare's comedies."[13] *The Flower of Friendshippe* is interesting also in revealing Tyllney's ability to capitalize on what he perceived to be the court's taste. A comment by one of the major characters in Tyllney's book indicates that the court was enthralled by the Continental *conversazione* and was imitating the form in their own pastimes. Tyllney creates a discourse in this form: he relies on, even mentions both Castiglione's *The Courtier* and Boccaccio's *Filocopo,* both of which had recently been translated into English, creates the characters of Erasmus and Vives (the first appearance in English fiction of historical personages as characters), and names his chief character Pedro de Lujan after the author of his main source, *Coloquios matrimoniales.*[14] Tyllney employs all of the devices of rhetoric at his disposal to resolve the apparent contradictions of marriage in an ideal vision of harmony. The court found the work so attractive that it went through four and possibly five editions within ten years and still another edition was issued in 1587. But Tyllney seems to have regarded his writing only in terms of its ability to get him the appointment he wanted for he never published anything again.

Lord Charles Howard maintained a company of players at court in the mid-1570s. They performed "Tooley" in 1576. "The Solitary Knight" in 1577, and a third play in 1578.[15] While there is no evidence to link Tyllney with the production of these particular plays, immediately after the company's last appearance at court he assumed his duties in the Revels Office. He served as Master, probably under a yearly commission from the Lord Chamberlain, until his formal appointment by patent on 24 July 1579.[16]

II

Tyllney was successful in handling the complex responsibilities of his position when the rest of Elizabeth's Masters of the Revels failed because of his unique blend of administrative and aesthetic talents. There had been widespread dissatisfaction with almost every facet of the office since the time of Henry VIII which steadily grew in intensity until the early 1570s. After Sir Thomas Benger's death in 1572 no patent was issued to a new Master; oversight of the office was entrusted to the heads of other household departments and, eventually, to the Clerk, Thomas Blagrave, who operated the office under a yearly commission from the Lord Chamberlain. Dissatisfaction reached crisis proportions in 1573 and memoranda detailing solutions to the problems of the office were solicited from all of the inferior officers.[17] Their recommendations ranged from schemes to reduce expenses, a particularly pressing issue, to suggestions that a "man of credit" be found to take over the Mastership. Tyllney proved, in fact, to be that "man of credit" and spent fifteen years reorganizing the office, building it into the powerful and efficient instrument by which the central government exercised its control over the drama in all of its forms throughout the realm.

Part of the problem with the Revels organization was the schedule itself. The season began in early November when the Master and his officers previewed the plays in contention for presentation that year in full dress rehearsals at their office in St. John's. Selection was made, the texts "reformed" (i.e., rewritten or altered) to suit the court's taste, and productions planned. Material would then be procured, either from other household departments or purchased on credit, artisans would be hired and their work of fashioning the elaborate costumes, massive scenery, and ornate stage properties would be supervised. All of the material would then be transported, usually by barge, to wherever the court was spending the season. The production then had to be erected in the Great Hall of that palace and lighting, designed by the officers and fashioned by the "wiredrawers," had to be installed. All of this had to be accomplished between early November and late December when the officers personally supervised their first production. Anywhere from eight to fourteen performances were given during the season and much of the same procedure was followed for each. After the entertainment, the equipment was disassembled and transported back to St. John's where it was used for later productions (the necessary alterations being made to disguise the fact) or stored for future use. After Ash Wednesday, the traditional end of the revels season, the duties of the officers slacked off until the twenty-day "airing" period during the summer when they took inventory and cleaned out and aired the properties.

One of the major problems produced by this tight schedule under the earlier Masters was dull plays. Blagrave, acting Master for the season of 1573–74, put on Mulcaster's Children in "Timoclea at the Siege of Thebes," which the court found so tedious that the scheduled masque afterwards was cancelled.[18] There was simply not enough control over the kind of plays being written for the acting companies, over the amount of practice they could get, and over the workmen and material that the officers could command when they needed them. And there was obviously little time to remedy the situation. The major innovation introduced under Tyllney's Mastership to deal with the first two problems was the creation of the Queen's Company of Players. Elizabeth did have a company of "interluders" which she inherited from the previous reign but she made little use of them, preferring her Masters to arrange performances by the children or adult companies. In 1584 Tyllney received authorization to organize the Queen's Men which he did by raiding the existing companies for twelve of the finest actors of the day, all sworn as Grooms of the Chamber and paid livery and wages accordingly.[19] He seems to have worked closely with the company, probably both on the material that they played and on the amount of practice they had, for during the next decade Tyllney had them present anywhere from two to five of the plays put on for the court during each season. And we hear no further in the records about the court's boredom.

From the point of view of those responsible for fiscal management, the main problem with the Revels Office was its enormous expense. Tyllney spent a good amount of time during his early Mastership traveling to the court to consult with Lord Burghley and with the Queen about his plans for reorganization. His solution to the problem had an important bearing on the later relationship between dramatists and the court. For Tyllney relied on the play rather than on the masque as the mainstay of his entertainment schedule.

The masque was introduced as an attempt to enhance the brilliance of Henry VIII's court by imitating fashionable Continental revels. Edward Hall described the first entertainment of this type given on Twelfth Night, 1512, when the king and eleven companions were disguised in the manner of Italy, "a thyng not seen afore in Englande." The novelty lay in the dancing of disguised persons with members of the audience. But this new form was comfortably integrated with the multiform spectacles that William Cornish had already produced at court combining music, poetry, *débat,* combat, scenic display, and dance. The Henrican entertainment, combining both English and Continental devices, was the ancestor of the masques that reached their height of splendor at the courts of James I and Charles I.[20] Even in Elizabeth's reign when masques were not as elaborate as they were at her father's—or were to be again at King James's—court, plays were far less expensive to produce. Early in Elizabeth's reign virtually all of the entertainments presented at court were masques. In 1567 plays begin to dominate but masques still account for one-third to one-half of the schedule. In the 1573–74 season Blagrave furnished six plays and three masques under the Revels budget at a cost of £721 14s

2d, an average of roughly £80 each. In contrast, during Tyllney's first regular season as Master in 1579–80, he produced nine plays at a cost of £261 15s 2d, or an average of roughly £29 each.[21] The distinction between the play as an ordinary expense of the office and the masque as an extraordinary one, clearly developing since the beginning of Tyllney's Mastership as part of a financial reform, was firmly established by the 1590s and at King James's court the vastly expensive masques were no longer considered the province of the Revels Office but were under the supervision of the Lord Chamberlain and Master of the Horse. Masque writers and producers like Ben Jonson and Inigo Jones were commissioned directly by members of the court, not by the Revels Office.

Lack of control over workmen and material for the entertainments was also a problem which had an important bearing on the finances of the office. The Exchequer was so slow in paying its bills that sometimes two years elapsed before creditors received payment for goods and services. In self-defence the merchants charged the office a third more than retail price in an attempt to cover the losses they sometimes suffered by having to sell their bills to speculators at half-price. This problem was remedied by granting Tyllney a special commission in 1581 which allowed him to impress workmen and material at "fair prices" and to protect his workmen from arrest during the period of their service. But this "totalitarian authority," as Boas described it, over goods and services was the concern of only the first half of the commission.[22] The second half, in effect, made Tyllney theatrical censor of the realm. He was charged to examine, alter, and allow or suppress every play written for public performance.

Tyllney's position as censor was perhaps the most anxiety-provoking aspect of his duties for it placed him squarely at the center of the powerful and competing interests that surrounded the drama. The Queen and the court demanded sophisticated entertainment and this meant that acting companies had to be provided with conditions which were favorable to the production of new scripts and which allowed them sufficient practice. The Privy Council, bowing to the Queen's wishes, supported the players but had reservations of its own about the political expedience of allowing them a free hand and worked sometimes through Tyllney and sometimes on its own to censor plays. The London City Corporation objected to playing on social and moral grounds. From their point of view the playhouses were health hazards in providing the conditions for the spread of plague, social evils in providing opportunities for criminals to gather and unrest to ferment, and morally debilitating to individuals in distracting attention either from work during the week or from worship on Sunday. They were never satisfied with anything short of complete suppression of the theaters, as their letters and petitions to the Privy Council and the Archbishop of Canterbury reveal. The Archbishop, as chief religious censor, was himself concerned about the open discussion of religious matters on stage. Tyllney was alternately the instrument and target of policy for all of these special interest groups, continually challenged to balance the tensions that surrounded the issue. Further, he had a personal stake in the matter; he derived an income from the licensing of manuscripts and from the theaters themselves and he was continually alert to preserve that income.[23]

III

Tyllney's reputation steadily grew after his appointment as Master of the Revels. In 1581 he had been mentioned by the Spanish Ambassador as a possible envoy to Spain and while he does not ever seem to have served in this capacity, the fact that he was considered is sufficient to indicate his reputation in diplomatic circles.[24] While never knighted, Tyllney was entitled to be marshalled with knights in virtue of his Mastership. He marched with Bachelor Knights in the 24 November 1588 procession celebrating the defeat of the Spanish Armada.[25] Later, his precedence was apparently challenged on the grounds that he was only an esquire, but the College of Heralds confirmed his official position with knights on 18 March 1600.[26] Perhaps encouraged by his early successes and recognition as well as attracted by the prospect of a good match he applied for a license on 4 May 1583 to marry Dame Mary Bray, a daughter of Sir Thomas Cotton and fourth wife, now widow, of Sir Edward Bray.[27] Sir Edward died in 1581, leaving his entire estate in Surrey "without impeachment of any waste" to her on the condition that after her death the estate would pass eventually to his grandson, Edward Bray.[28] Tyllney's marriage lasted for twenty-one years; there were no children. Mary died on 20 February 1604 and was buried beside her first husband.[29]

In 1589, with the income from his Surrey and Middlesex lands, Tyllney purchased the largest house in Leatherhead, Surrey, where he was visited by the Queen during her summer progress on 3 August 1591.[30] By 1594 he was the largest landholder in the parish, holding £25 of assessed land, and began to assume the responsibilities associated with one of the county's leading citizens.[31] He was continually active in local politics for close to two decades: he was one of the assessors for the second lay subsidy in Surrey in 1594, one of the justices for the middle division in the county in 1605, and a letter from Tyllney to Sir William More indicates that he was well informed about the issues being discussed at the county sessions and also that he had been involved in a number of confrontations with officials about local matters.[32]

By the early 1590s Tyllney was a veteran of a number of law suits. These suits fall into three classes: those involving his difficulties in asserting his ownership of the lands and manors left to his wife by Sir Edward Bray; those stemming from his joint executorship, along with his cousin Phillip, of the will of John Digges; and miscellaneous suits over the purchases of property.[33] He managed eventually to get legal possession for a time of his wife's Surrey lands, for it was with the income from these that he purchased his house in Leatherhead. The Middlesex land came, in part, from the estate of Digges. Digges, a merchant tailor, employee of the Revels Office from 1579 until his death in 1584/85, was described by the opposition in these suits as a thief, a shifter, "named and reputed to be one Tyllney's bastard," who died in "Mr. Tyllney's house in St. Iohns." The legal entanglements of the estate involved a complicated battery of suits and countersuits pursued in chancery, star chamber, common law, and the court of requests over bonds that Digges had signed for his own debts and as surety for his friends, and over land that he had given to Tyllney in Middlesex. All of this was further complicated by conspiracies on the part of deedholders, bondholders, and other executors to cash in on the estate.

There were personal hostilities as well. Phillip Tyllney's son, Charles, was involved in the conspiracy to overthrow Elizabeth and place Mary Queen of Scots in the throne, an involvement which got him executed with Babington in 1586. The fact that Charles admitted to discussing the Queen's murder despite his insistence that he did not consent, as well as his adherence to the Catholic faith, was enough to convict him as an accessory and guilty of treason.[34] Charles died proclaiming his faith, praying for the Queen in Latin, and warning all young men to take example about their companions from him. He owed £200 to £300 at his death, which he requested his friends to pay. But the burden probably fell on his father, who in one of the suits over Digges's estate seems to have taken revenge for his son. Raffe Bott testified in a Star Chamber suit that both Phillip and Edmond "thyrsted and longyed to be revengd on him" for they believed he had custody of Charles during his imprisonment in the Tower.[35]

Tyllney filed suits himself to recover land in Hertfordshire and in Surrey and to recover a forfeited £100 bond from Phillip Henslowe, proprietor of the Rose Theater, and Francis Langley, proprietor of the Swan. Despite his land holdings, his income from his post as Master, and his licensing fees, Tyllney did not have a comfortable enough income. By 1601 he was in deep financial trouble. His cousin, Thomas, paid him fifty marks a year from this time until his death on the promise that Edmond would bequeath him his land property. Thomas stated in a later Chancery deposition that he had paid this money so that Edmond would not be forced to sell his house and land to maintain himself.[36] Thomas does not seem to exaggerate, for on 20 October 1607 Tyllney was sued by Elizabeth Cartwright from whom he had purchased his house in Leatherhead for £100 and an annuity of £15. Presumably Edward Bray recovered all of the inheritance from his grandfather's estate after Tyllney's wife died depriving Edmond of the income from those Surrey lands that he had been using to pay Elizabeth. Further, after Phillip Tyllney's death in 1602, the family lost land in Lincolnshire to Sir George Buc who sued for those lands as next of kin to Phillip's mother.

IV

The accounts from Tyllney's Mastership indicate that he liked to be at court. He attended far more often than his inferior officers and made a practice of bringing a doorkeeper and three other attendants with him. He owned a wardrobe so elaborate that he felt compelled to repent it in his will, and apparently the burlesque of the court officers in the Gray's Inn entertainment of 1594 was not far from the truth—which singled out the Master of the Revels as a conspicuous figure at court entertainments.[37] There was not at Elizabeth's court, as there was at many other European courts, a Master of Ceremonies, whose duty it was to entertain foreign ambassadors at the official spectacles. The Lord Chamberlain arranged their precedence and personally, along with his aides, entertained them. No doubt Tyllney was called upon to help in this matter.

Perhaps because of his successes at court but also because of his growing financial problems, Tyllney began to prepare for a higher position, probably for something equivalent to a Master of Ceremonies. He approached the matter in the way he had earlier prepared for the Mastership of the Revels, by writing a work for his sovereign and by enlisting the support of the Howards. This time, rather than a literary work, he prepared the confidential, diplomatic reference work, the "Topographical Descriptions." The manuscript, a massive production of over a quarter of a million words, surveyed diplomatically valuable information about the eight major countries in Europe and was designed as an aid in conducting foreign policy. Both internal and external evidence suggest that he made the decision to go ahead with this work in the late 1590s. His earlier notes for the work were updated with sources not in print until the 1590s. And the Revels Office, perhaps as early as 1589, had adopted a new system of finance by which the officers were paid a flat fee for their attendance at work and at court, and by 1595–97 Tyllney had been involved in a five-year dispute with his officers over the amount each was to be paid in wages.[38] Lord Burghley eventually had to send in a Auditor and a Barron of the Exchequer to force an agreement; in the settlement Tyllney lost about £10 a year in income. Both the income and the climate were uncomfortable enough to make the office less than attractive. It was also in 1597 that the reversion of Tyllney's patent became an issue. John Lyly, the dramatist, expected the reversion. He appears to have had something in the way of a promise from the Queen herself and in his letters he mentions that he had waited for the post for thirteen years.[39] By 1597 it was clear to Lyly that George Buc was a serious contender for the office. It seems that Tyllney prepared his manuscript for presentation to the Queen as part of a move, backed by Howard, now Earl of Nottingham, to assure both of them positions at court: Buc as Master of the Revels and Tyllney as Master of Ceremonies. No assurance was given either to Buc or to Tyllney during Elizabeth's reign; in fact, Tyllney did not present his manuscript to the Queen at all. But his hopes were still alive in 1603; he revised sections of the manuscript after the Queen's death and added a dedication to King James. But the manuscript does not seem to have been presented to the King either. James did create the position of Master of Ceremonies but it was given to Sir Lewis Leuknor, translator of Contarini's *Commonwealth and Government of Venice* (1595), because of his "good education and experience" and instruction in foreign languages, on 21 May 1603 at a fee of £200 a year.[40] It appears that Tyllney abandoned work on his manuscript at this point. Buc, of course, did receive the reversion of Tyllney's patent over all contenders, but since Tyllney was still in office Buc had to involve himself in Howard's service and in licensing plays for publication until Tyllney died.

His wife died around the time of this major disappointment but Tyllney still continued to be active in local politics and in the Revels Office; he personally attended at the office and at court throughout the Revels season of 1609–10.[41] He died on 20 August 1610 after an illness.[42] In his will he settled his outstanding debts, gave liberally to the poor, to his relatives, and his friends, bequeathed his house to his cousin, Thomas, as he had promised, and hoped to be saved by Christ "vnto everlastinge liefe accordinge vnto his promise vnto all such as trewlie and vnfeignedlie beleeve in him." He wished to be buried like his grandfather, "withoute any ffunerall pompe or charge other then a Sermon," and at St. Leonard's Church, "'neare vnto the Monument of my ffather, longe since buried there."[43]

II
Topographical Descriptions, Regiments, and Policies

THE TITLE OF TYLLNEY'S WORK, "Topographical Descriptions, Regiments, and Policies . . . ," is somewhat misleading. Strictly speaking, topography is concerned with the detailed description of the surface features of an area, its mountains, rivers, bridges, roads, towns, etc. In practice, sixteenth-century topographies or surveys were more inclusive. They relied for method on contemporary chorography, a genre concerned with depicting history and geography, but which included, in a somewhat random manner, heraldic and genealogical information and accounts of distinctive cultural features, such as fairs, ceremonies, and festivals, associated with the area described. Tyllney's work was, in fact, a reaction against the detailed description and amorphous organization of the topographies of the period, which he felt were unsuitable for diplomatic purposes. He complains in the dedication to King James that these works provided only a "Geographicall" understanding of the countries surveyed. His method of collecting information was that recommended by Secretary Davison at the end of his list of instructions:

> Besides these three [the country, the people, the government] occure many other things to bee obserued as the Mint, valuation of coines, exchanges with infinite other particularities which for brevities sake I omit and which yourselfe by diligent reading, observation, and conference may easily supply.[1]

Tyllney reduced to essential details a vast amount of information derived from his reading in contemporary printed sources, private manuscripts, confidential government documents, and from conferences with well-informed sources on the geography, history, law, government, politics, genealogy, peerage, chronologies, military fortifications, chief families, coats of arms, and the temper of the people and princes of Europe. He refused to discuss the Reformation, leaving the matter, as he says "vnto any Person off greater Experiens, and sounder Iudgmentt". The resulting work embodies features distinct enough to classify the manuscript as topography, as political description, or as heraldic compilation. But the manuscript is rather an amalgam of all of these "types," presented in a highly organized form, a unique reference work, created to fill a particular need. Tyllney continued to collect notes over the years, haphazardly it seems, for he mentions that it was difficult to decide on an organization for the material derived from the "Intricated laborynth" of sources that he studied. It appears that he began in earnest to write a draft for the manuscript in 1597 but the project was not brought to its present state of completion until after James's accession in 1603.

An organization and indexing system was of paramount importance if the manuscript was to succeed as a diplomatic reference work. Tyllney decided to concentrate his efforts on those countries which he had "most trauailed in" and to settle on "one Vniform Methode" through them all. He divided his manuscript into eight books, each of which treated one of the countries or major areas of Europe: Italy, France, Germany together with Switzerland, Poland, Hungary, and Denmark; The Netherlands; Spain together with Portugal; England together with Wales; Scotland; and Ireland together with the Isles of Man, Wight, Jersey, and Guernsey. The "Vniform Methode" involved dividing each of these books into four major parts: the first part described the national state and government; in the second, the country was divided into regions and each of those areas was described; then, a brief chronology of the monarchs of the country was provided; finally, the emblazoned arms of the chief families of the nation were provided along with brief notes about them.

The beginning chapter of each book describes the national state. The information provided includes the derivation of the country's ancient name, a historical discussion of its borders, its present size and bordering countries, the number of cities, towns, and universities within it, the people who have historically inhabited it, their principal occupations, and an assessment of their national character. The second chapter is devoted to a description of the courses of the major navigable rivers. The third provides a historical discussion of the central government. Other chapters in this section are concerned with a description of the various courts, their system of pleading, their staffs and wages; the main sources of the nation's revenue, its amount, and how it is spent also occupies a chapter. Sometimes in this section and at others at the end of the second section, a chapter is provided explaining the historical development of peerage titles as well as information on the number of able-bodied men capable of being mustered for service.

In the second section of each book the country is subdivided into regions or provinces and several chapters are devoted to each region. The beginning of the first chapter provides essentially the same information included in the first chapter on the national state: the ancient name of the region, its boundaries, its chief commodities, its people. Then follows a series of brief topographical descriptions of the major cities, towns, and castles, focusing on their chief governmental, military, economic, and cultural features. The chapter concludes with a general description of the economic strengths and weaknesses of the region and a detailed list of the chief landholders and nobility who have influence in the area. Following this initial chapter are usually several short chapters which provide genealogies of the chief peers of the region. After all of the provinces of the country are described in this manner a brief chapter concludes the section by describing the export-import relationship of the country with England and other countries.

Except in the case of Ireland and the Netherlands, a chronology of the countries' monarchs comprises the third section of the books. There are brief notes on the individual reigns of the monarchs, including the dates of each king's reign and his age at death. All of the books conclude with a section in which the coats of arms of the most ancient families are emblazoned. Tyllney used special leaves with printed rules for this purpose. Each leaf could accommodate forty coats of arms within neat border rules and above each coat there is a space ruled for a brief note on the family.

Besides a clearly defined overall organization Tyllney was careful to provide the work with a system of indexes. The preliminary material to the manuscript serves as an introduction to the purposes of the work. This preliminary material, which appears in the form of four tables in F1, is revealing of Tyllney's hopes for the work. He begins by distinguishing between types of government—monarchy, aristocracy, and democracy. In a thoroughly orthodox treatment, the strengths and weaknesses of each type are discussed; democracy is despised as a government "full of ignorance and confusion" and monarchy preferred for its resemblance to the "divine regiment of God."

Having thus established the superiority of monarchy, Tyllney in the next chart focuses on the best policy for managing the government. Good relations with bordering countries, good internal management of the commonwealth, and an equitable legal system are encouraged by leagues, marriages of state, representative government, sound laws, and the indifferent administration of justice. These first two charts contain perfectly ordinary treatments of their respective subjects. The classification of government is not original with Tyllney nor new to the Renaissance. It is derived ultimately from Aristotle's *Politics* and in one form or another is discussed by virtually every political theorist following him.[2] The characteristics of good government are also sentiments so thoroughly diffused in the Renaissance that Tyllney might easily have constructed the chart from the commonplaces of court conversation.

In contrast to the first two charts, which are influenced by political treatises in general, the next two are influenced by the intelligence instruction genre. The natural situation of the country, its chief strengths, its accessibility to aid in time of crisis, its temporal and ecclesiastical order, the chief trades of its common people, their loyalty to the prince, economic status, political leanings, and the extent and kind of their military training is the concern of the third chart. The fourth attempts to classify the attributes of sovereign magistrates according to their gifts of fortune and of mind. The sovereign's virtues and vices and income and expenses are listed in outline form. And while the charts are more revealing of Tyllney's own hopes for the uses to which his manuscript could be put, they occupy much space and set out in detail commonplaces that his intended users could well do without.

Tyllney himself realized this and abandoned the detailed chart for a much simplified version which occupies only the title page of F2. The new chart, which very much resembles the overall division of Secretary Davison's list of instructions, indicates that information is to be found in three main categories: the description of the country, the worth of the people, and the ability of the prince.

The revision of the preliminary material for F2 is characteristic of Tyllney's attempt to make the material in his manuscript readily accessible. The manuscript is provided with a table of contents which includes the folio numbers of each of its books. Similarly, each of the eight books has its own table of contents. The complex second section of each of the books, in which the country is subdivided into regions, opens with a brief index to its contents. Finally, each of the books is provided with a general index. That Tyllney was concerned about the reliability of his indexing system is indicated by the fact that he personally wrote the indexes for France, Germany, and Scotland in F2 and filled in the folio numbers for virtually all of the tables of contents and the remaining indexes himself.

Tyllney points out in his dedication that the work was intended for the King's use as a "Breuiate vnto your Highnes Memorie, for matters of chiffest Note therin, vppon any suddaine." It was a reference guide for use in conducting foreign policy which Tyllney considered too sensitive to be published "vnto the Common Vew, and Censure of the ignorantt." This massive production, containing over a quarter of a million words, over two thousand coats of arms, and over one hundred engravings and maps, probably never served the purpose for which it was intended; nevertheless, it provides us with the most complete contemporary description of Europe during the reign of Elizabeth extant in the language and a heroic example of an attempt to give shape to intelligence material, including everything that an informed member of the English court thought diplomatically valuable.

II

To illustrate his description of Europe Tyllney included a number of maps, engravings, and coats of arms. Two types of maps are included.[5] The large folding maps of Europe and of each of the countries described are colored engravings which he probably bought from a dealer. These maps have been folded and tipped to the stubs of leaves cut for the purpose at the beginning of each of the books. The small maps of the countries, tipped into the margins of the description of England and Wales in F1, were cut from the earliest pack of geographical playing cards produced in England; they were not included in F2. With the exception of the folding map of Scotland, all of the maps included in F2 differ from those in F1. Several of the maps are rare and four of them are unique. Peter van den Keere's *Hyberniae* (1591) from F1, and his *Angliae Regnum* (ca. 1600) from F2, are each one of only two known copies of these maps. The maps of Italy, France, Germany, and Spain from F2 were all printed by Peter Overadt, a Cologne dealer in engravings and a publisher. These unique maps, printed in 1598, antedate all of Overadt's previously known work. They are elaborately, although not finely, engraved and include portraits of the chief monarchs of each country as well as emblematic engravings and verses, suggesting that they may have been part of a larger series. The maps of France, Germany, and Italy are copies after Gerard Mercator's *Galliae Tabule Geographice* (Duysburgi, 1585), *Germania Tabule Geographice* (Duysburgi, 1585), and *Italiae, Sclavoniae, et Graciae Tabule Geographice* (Duysburgi, 1589); Spain is a copy of Ortelius's *Regni Hispaniae* from *Theatrum*

Orbis Terrarum (1570).

Fifty-four engraved portraits are included in F1 and 110 in F2. Forty-six of these portraits, forty in F1 and six in F2, were probably purchased from a dealer in flat sheets, then cut to size and tipped into the texts and to the backs of the maps. These portraits of the chief temporal and ecclesiastical princes of Europe illustrate most of the books in F1 but Tyllney acquired only enough new portraits for Italy and England in F2. As part of his effort to prepare F2 for presentation to King James, Tyllney included three unique portraits of the King by Benjamin Wright. The majority of the engravings are small portraits, "Medalias to the Liffe" as Tyllney calls them, of the Roman Emperors from Julius Caesar to Rudolph II, which are used to illustrate the chronologies of Italy and Germany. The full set of 104 portraits is contained in F2; only fourteen survive in the fragment of the German chronology in F1. These portraits may have been commissioned especially by Tyllney for the project. The practice was common enough; Harrison had a similar plan for the Kings of England in his projected Chronology.

The 2,556 coats of arms in F1 and the 2,126 coats in F2 make the manuscript one of the largest compilations of arms from the period. Artists were hired to hand-paint these arms into the manuscript and, in some instances, Tyllney's blazoning instructions in pencil are still visible—*a* = argent [silver, white, or page background], *b* = azure, *g* = gules, *o* = or [gold or yellow], *p* = purpure, and *s* = sable. The arms illustrate the title pages and the margins of the texts, but most are included in the catalogues of the chief families that conclude each of the books.

III
Historical and Literary Significance of the Work

I

WHILE TRAVEL HAD BEEN emphasized as an educational experience since Chaucer's time, it was not until the sixteenth century with the increased interest in exploration, the influence of international Humanism in education, and England's own emergence from her intestine broils that travel received widespread approval as an essential part of a well-rounded education. Beginning in 1575 with the translation of Jerome Turler's *The Traveler,* to be followed throughout the century by many books in the same vein, the benefits of travel experience were made available to a public only too willing to read about it. Objections were still raised; men like Asham, ironically himself a traveler, who considered experience the schoolhouse of fools and ill men, carried on the debate over the debilitating effects of travel experience until well into the seventeenth century. But the bulk of the argument, especially among those who aspired to public office, was on the side of experience, and the groundwork for what was later to become known as the *Grand Tour* was already in formation. Gabriel Harvey in his own copy of *The Traveler,* a gift from Edmund Spenser, underlined the passage: "Experience is the greatest parte of humane wisedome, and the same is increased by traueil."[1] And by 1633 when Benjamin Fisher took up the argument he expressed what had been the opinion of the politically astute for many years:

> It hath bin lately maintained in an Academical Dispute that the best trayninge is in maps and good authors: because thereby a man may take a view of the state and manner of the whole world, and never mix with the corruptions of it . . . indeed, it is a good way to keepe a man innocent; but withall as Ignorantt. Our sedentary traueller may appear for a wise man, as Long as he conuerseth with dead men by reading; or writing, with men absent. But let him once enter on the stage of public employment, and he will soon find, if he can bee but sensible of contempt, that he is unfit for Action.[2]

Seasoning the judgement of the individual was only half the issue. The other function that travel experience served was to provide intelligence information for the state. In an age without fully developed information networks, intelligence came primarily from travelers, and especially, although not exclusively,[3] from those who were connected with the court. Collecting intelligence is as old as political organization and Turler cites the instruction Moses gave "them whom hee sent to viewe the lande of Chanaan" as a historical precedent to recommend it.[4] But it was not until the third quarter of the sixteenth century, if we can believe Turler's claim that he was first to make this information public, that detailed sets of recommendations for the systematic collection of intelligence became available.[5] Phillip Jones in his translation of Albert Meier's *Certain briefe and special Instructions . . .* , illustrates the need for these recommendations with an anecdote:

> I haue heard speech of a wise Gentlemen of Naples whom sometime for a triall dismissed his son, and gaue him libertie to trauell to certaine other cities, and territories of Italy, but without instruction and vpon his return, he made report that he had seene men and women, wals, houses, woods, and meadows, but of the state, manners, Lawes, governments and natures of the people his simple wit could make no reasonable answer. Many of our own nation have been taken tardy and tripping in this grosseness.[6]

One of those Englishmen "taken tardy" was Sir Phillip Sidney, whose guilt feelings over his own wasted travel are expressed in a letter of instructions to his brother. He laments how much he missed for "want of having directed my course to the right end and by the right means."[7] The right end, as he goes on to explain, was "to furnish yourself with the knowledge of such things as may be serviceable to your country." The right means were detailed lists of instructions on what to observe, as the ones he gives to his brother in this letter.

At first, the instruction gap in England was filled by translations of Continental works; later in the century books by Englishmen begin to dominate the field. An example of how seriously these travel instructions were taken is provided by Gabriel Harvey's reading list. In addition to Turler, he seems to have read Zwinger's *Methodus Apedemica* (Basel, 1577), Bourne's *Treasure for Travelers* (London, 1578), Guevara's *Art of Navigation,* tr. Edward Hellowes (London, 1578), Meier's *Certaine Briefe and Special Instructions,* tr. Phillip Jones (London, 1589), to name only a few of the most prominent. The genre developed throughout the century from discursive treatments of the value of travel both to individuals and the state, supported by classical precedents and *exempla,* to more detailed and more technical lists of instructions which assume their value as already proven. Robert Tanner, for example, dedicated his *Mirror for Mathematiques* to Tyllney's patron, Lord Charles Howard, in 1587; this work sets out the mathematical methods by which a traveler could measure the dams, harbors, and fortifications of foreign princes.

Intelligence, of course, was collected by Englishmen before the activity was popularized in the later sixteenth century and the kinds of information they did collect indicates that these published accounts, while more elaborate in detail, were built around a basic core of chorographical, topographical, and genealogical information that had been collected all along. The journal of Richard Smith, who traveled with Sir Edward Unton to Italy in 1563, shows what careful attention he paid to the fortifications, fertility of the provinces, nature of the inhabitants, and principal commodities.[8] Advice to travelers before the published lists of instructions were available was supplied by private letters. But even after the published lists were available it was still accepted practice for those who wished their accounts to be taken seriously, like Sidney's brother, to seek advice from experienced politicians and courtiers. Many of these letters of advice survive from the period, the most famous of which was Lord Burghley's instructions to the Earl of Rutland.[9] Indeed, even some of the most influential books of instructions translated into English were manuscripts either commissioned by or dedicated to Continental nobility. Jones notes in the preface to his translation of Meier's *Certain Instructions* that he wrote the book "at the command, direction and charge of the honorable Henry Ranzou, now lord of Bredenberge, Counsailer and deputie to Christern, the young King of Denmark"; Turler dedicated his own book to the three young Barons of Schonburg.[10]

One of the most detailed private lists of instruction that survives from the period is attributed to Secretary William Davison (ca. 1595).[11] It is important because it reveals what intelligence was particularly desirable at higher levels at the English court. Davison divides the information to be collected into three broad categories: the people, the country, and the policy and government. While it is a long list, it is worth quoting in its entirety.

In the Country you are to consider:

I. The situation and nature thereof, as whether it be: 1. Island or continent; near or far from the sea. 2. Plain or hilly; full or scarce of rivers.

II. Quantity: 1. Length. 2. Breadth. 3. Circuit. Where also the: A. Form. B. Climate.

III. How it confineth with other Countries and: 1. What these Countries are. 2. What their strength and riches are. 3. Wherein they consist. 4. Whether friends or enemies.

IV. The fertility thereof, and what commodities it doth either: 1. Yield and bring forth, and what part thereof hath been or is: A. consumed at home. B. vented abroad. 2. Want, and how and from whence it is supplied.

NATURE

V. Of what strength it is and how defended against the attempts of bordering neighbors, either by: 1. Sea, where may be observed what: A. Ports and havens it hath and of what: i. Access. ii. Capacity. iii. Traffick. iv. Shipping. B. Other Defence upon the coast. 2. Land, what: A. Mountains. B. Rivers. C. Marshes. D. Woods.

ART—As what cities, towns, castles, etc. it hath either within the land or upon the frontiers and how they are 1. Fortified. 2. Peopled.

VI. What universities or places of learning it hath and of what: 1. Foundation. 2. Revenue. 3. Profession.

VII. What Countries and Provinces are subject thereunto and what: 1. The same contain in: A. Quantity. B. Quality. 2. The People are for: A. Number. B. Affection. 3. The form of government and by whom administered.

Secondly, is to be considered the People

I. Their number: as whether they be A. Many.B. Few.

II. Quality: as their trade and kind of life whereunto they give themselves and whereby they live; as whether by: 1. Exercise of: A. Mechanical arts and merchandises. B. Husbandry. C. Arms. 2. Their rents and revenues.

III. Kinds and degrees: 1. Natives: A. Noble. B. Not noble. 2. Strangers: A. Denizens. B. Not denizens.

NOBLE

Generally as their: 1. Number. 2. Quality and degree of nobility. 3. Residence and place of abode. 4. Religion. 5. Gifts of body and mind where also their: A. Virtues. B. Vices. C. Studies. D. Exercises. 6. Profession of life: A. Civil. B. Material. 7. Means wherein are: A. Their revenues and comings in. B. Their issuings and goings out. 8. Offices and Authority they bear in the State. 9. Credit and favor or disfavor with the: A. Prince. B. People, and upon what cause. 10. Factions and partialities if any be, with the grounds, causes, and proceedings thereof.

Particularly as their: 1. Original, antiquity, arms. 2. Names and titles of dignities. 3. Alliances, offsprings, genealogies.

Thirdly, the Policy and government

In the policy and government falleth to be considered I. The Laws whereby it is governed. II.

Persons that govern. In the laws you have to note:

I. Their kinds as 1. Civil. 2. Canon or municipal.

II. Their conformity with the nature of the people. The persons that govern are the magistrates: 1. Sovereign. 2. Subalternal. The Sovereign is either: 1. One as a monarch. 2. More as: A. Optimates or Magnates. B. Popular.

In the former may be comprehended: I. the means whereby he attaineth the same, whether there by sovereignty as: 1. Succession. 2. Election. 3. Usurpation. II. How he doth carry himself in administration thereof, where may be observed: 1. His Court. 2. His wisdom. 3. His inclination to: A. Peace. B. War. 4. How he is beloved or feared of his: A. People. B. Neighbors. 5. His designments, enterprizes, etc. 6. His disposition, studies, and exercises of: A. Body. B. Mind. 7. His favorites. 8. The confidence or distrust he hath in his people.

In things that concern his estate fall cheifly to be considered: 1. His reveneues: A. Ordinary. B. Extraordinary, abroad and at home. In his friends and confederacies you are to consider how and upon what respects they are leagued with him; what help, succor, and commodity he hath had, or expecteth from them, and upon what ground. His power and strength for offence and defence are to be measured by the: 1. Strength of his Country. 2. Number and quality of his forces for: A. Nature. 2. Art. 3. Commanders. 4. Soldiers: A. Horse. B. Foot. 5. Magazine and provisions for his wars either by: A. Sea. B. Land. 6. Wars he hath made in times past to be considered the: A. Time. B. Cause. C. Precedency. D. Success.

The subaltern magistrate is either: 1. Ecclesiastical 2. Civil. Under the titles of ecclesiastical magistrate you may note: 1. The religion publicly professed; the form and government of the church. 2. The persons employed therein as: A. Archbishops. B. Bishops. C. Deans. D. Abbots: i. number ii. degree iii. offices iv. authority v. qualities vi. revenues.

The civil magistrates subalternate are those which under the soveraign have administration of: 1. The state. 2. Justice. Among the magistrates that have the managing of the state follow cheifly to be considered: I. The Council of Estate: 1. ordinary, attending on the princes person as the: A. Great Council B. Privy Council C. Cabnit Council. 2. Extraordinary, as the estates of parliament: A. Their number B. Their quality, as: i. place and authorite in council. ii. their wisdome. iii. fidelity. iv. credit and favor with the: a. Prince b. People. II. What Councils of—1. Finance. 2. Warres. 3. Provincials—he hath and by who administered. III. Lieutenants and Deputies of provinces employed either: 1. at home. 2. Abroad. IV. Officers, etc. 1. Admiralty. 2. Ordinance. V. Ambassadors public ministers and intelligemors [intelligence mongers?] employed with 1. Princes. 2. Commonwealths.

In the administration of Justice you have to consider: 1. The order and form observed in causes: 1. Civell 2. Criminall. II. The persons of the: 1. Presidents 2. Confederates 3. Advocats

It should be made clear that this list was not specifically designed to guide the kind of project Tyllney undertook. It was commonplace to recognize as Turler did that

> no one man . . . can obserue all thinges, muchless he that geueth himselfe wholy to some profession, or studieth some other thing, for which he hath traueiled. I grant it is true, nether writte I this to the ende that I would haue all men obserue all of them.[12]

The gathering of intelligence was thought to be a collective effort not an individual one. And indeed the intelligence circulating in the English court derived from a number of different sources and assumed different forms; letters, journals, captured documents, word of mouth report, notes from published books about foreign countries, all contributed in random ways to the body of knowledge available to decision makers on foreign policy. Late in the century there appears at least one document which suggests that there were attempts made to survey the "estate" of a foreign country in a systematic way. Confidential documents surveying the "estate" of England had regularly been produced throughout this period; the earliest I have personally examined dates from 1579; the latest from 1605.[13] These annual reports were copied out for most of the chief officers of state. The information included in them is in outline form; the worth of the various English bishoprics and the amount of money they paid annually in first fruits and tenths, the inventory and cost of maintaining the navy, the ordnance, the royal household, the garrison at Berwick and more are tabulated and organized for easy reference. Appended to one of these annual surveys (ca. 1595) is a description of the "estate" of Spain, modeled on the description of England.[14] A list of the Spanish bishops and nobility and their yearly worth, the provinces of the country and the amount they pay to the king in tribute, the king's ambassadors at foreign courts and their salaries, the number of ships in his navy, the amount of his revenue, the major cities of the country, the major navigable rivers, and more is provided in the same outline form as that of the estate of England. This attempt to organize intelligence about Spain into a practically usable form suggests that the need for convenient access to information about foreign countries was felt by more individuals at court than by Tyllney. He does not seem to have undertaken any project, and it is difficult to believe that he would have undertaken one as large and time consuming as the "Topographical

Descriptions," either without a careful investigation of the need for it or without advice on how to carry it out. Further, since he apparently pinned his hopes for promotion on the success of this work, it is reasonable to conclude that at least Lord Charles Howard, who had encouraged Robert Tanner in preparing the *Mirror for Mathematiques,* approved of the project.

II

Sidney advised his brother, in his letter of instruction, that the most important countries he should know were France, Spain, the Netherlands, and Germany. Tyllney seems to have been roughly in agreement, for France, Germany, the Netherlands, and Spain occupy the second through the fifth books of his manuscript. Scotland and Ireland, important because of their proximity to England, were described in the seventh and eighth books. But unlike Tyllney, Sidney did not consider Italy as important as the first four countries: "we know not what we haue, or can haue to do with them, but to buy their silkes and wines."[15] He did concede that information about Italy, as well as about the Turks, was important from a cultural standpoint. Tyllney seems to have included his brief description of Turkey as the final book of F1 for reasons similar to these, but decided to drop the book altogether for F2. Italy, however, he placed as the first book in the manuscript. In part, the reason for this prominent position was the attraction of writing about the influence of Roman institutions in contemporary Europe. But the main reasons for the importance of Italy were the authority of the Pope in politico-religious affairs, and the great influence of the King of Spain in Italian politics. Both of these factors were of great practical importance to Englishmen in the late sixteenth century.

At first glance it may not be apparent why Tyllney included a book on England in an intelligence manual designed for use at the English court. Anyone hoping to prepare a valuable intelligence report and anyone attempting to utilize the information in such a report must have a clear sense of the economic, political, and military institutions of his own country to make appropriate observations and comparisons. Tyllney's description of England is designed to make possible relevant comparisons between England and the most important of the Continental countries. His description, which occupies the sixth book of the manuscript, is arranged almost exactly as the Continental books are. England's history is critically reported. Tyllney gives an account of Samothes (one of the sons of Japhet) and his posterity who ruled England before Brute conquered the island:[16] "By the accompte of most writers who beleue ther was such a man . . . 2850 yeres after the creation of the world and 1116 yeres before the Incarnation of Christ." He is as even-handed in this treatment of the favorite myth that gave the British their distinguished heritage and consequently placed them in the same league with the Continent as he is in his treatment of the Plantagenet kings. He held these Angevin kings responsible for the internal strife which resulted in the loss of the bulk of England's possessions in France. The attitude toward history up to this point suggests that Tyllney saw individual actions rather than providence as responsible for the movement of history. Nevertheless, he is capable, when his passion is roused or when subscribing to an official line, of invoking the old providential scheme of history and was content, as were virtually all of his contemporaries, with the contradiction. He invokes a providential scheme often when discussing the interference of the Popes in political affairs and always when discussing the accession of Henry VII to the throne of England, healing the divisions between the houses of York and Lancaster, or of Queen Elizabeth, "last soueraigninge ouer the whole to the greate comfort of all her louinge subiects."

Natural and artificial fortifications are described, just as they are for the rest of the countries in Europe. The people were descended from the most warlike nations of the world and the country, surrounded by the sea, was "almost vnaccessable without greate and present daunger vnto the Invaders." The "politique" provisions for the country's safety included castles and special port towns along the southern coast, a navy of some "700 sail" (including 100 over 500 tons), and military training for civilians, modeled on the example of the ancient Romans, numbering 1,200,000 able-bodied men, a figure he seems to have calculated on his own.[17] His treatment of English political, economic, and legal institutions parallels that of the rest of the countries in Europe. The description of English law courts and their staffs and wages involves a historical discussion of the evolution of the law from Alfred the Great to the present. The description of the revenues and expenses of the crown and the Exchequer involves a historical discussion of the precedents for the various taxes, impositions, subsidies, and levies currently in use. The monarch's councils of state, the method of governing the realm, as well as the governments of the individual counties are provided with historical discussions also. The country is divided into regions by assembling the various provinces under the ancient Saxon kingdom to which they belonged, underscoring the antiquity of the country even further by providing their names in Saxon script, which he copied from Camden's *Britannia.*[18] Finally, in his description of the various ranks or degrees of the people of England he provides a historical discussion on the origin of titles. His description of England accomplishes two objectives. The historical discussions of the national myths, laws, titles, government, and revenue provide England with the same status, as far as its antique institutions are concerned, as the rest of Europe. Secondly, his even-handed treatment of English myth and his refusal to accept information uncritically enable him to be just as even-handed in his criticism of Continental institutions.

In the Continental books Tyllney is concerned to subject the history, government, legal system, economic organization, military preparation, princes, nobility, and citizens of the various countries to close inspection with the aim of revealing their weaknesses, strengths, and the possibility of a legitimate English claim to their territory. Tyllney especially admired France for its power, resources, and military provisions. Because of the ease with which it could be aided by Italy, Germany, and Switzerland he considered it the mightiest country in Europe. He was awed both by the "fearful" fortifications of its cities and castles and the "politique" provisions of its twelve governments for their security. Its people he considered valiant enough but so insolent that it was "allmoste not Tollerable amongeste Civill people." He deplored the legal system of pleading, modeled on Roman Law, as a "Contagious sickness," as he does almost every time he engages this issue in any of the books of the manuscript. While the people of France no longer enjoyed the freedom which they possessed under the "Frank Laws", they remained loyal to their king "aboue many Nations." This, Tyllney felt, was one of the chief reasons for the success of the French monarchy. He is particularly concerned to challenge at every opportunity the "Salik Law," which restricted succession to the French throne to the male line. He argues that the French themselves violated the Law twice: in 705 A.D. when Pepin deposed Childrick and again in 998 A.D. when Hugh Capet succeeded against Charles, Duke of Lorraine. He points out that Edward III was barred from the throne of France in favor of Philip of Valois by the French parliament and notes that Henry VI was crowned king of France in Paris in the fifteenth century. Tyllney was attracted to France not only because of the historical ties that existed between the two countries but also because the French had often found themselves at cross purposes with the Pope and the Spanish king. And any potential ally against Spain was of interest to England.

Germany, Tyllney felt, was a potentially powerful country but factiously divided by religious controversies and political jealousies. The continual struggles between Protestants and Catholics, between the nobility and citizens of the free cities for the control of the revenues of those cities, and especially the jealousy of the inferior princes of Germany for the House of Austria rendered the Emperor virtually impotent. His revenues were barely enough to support his court and ordinary obligations, and political jealousies in the Imperial Diets left him without the revenues needed even to maintain the integrity of his borders. Tyllney had a rather low opinion of the German people, soldiers, and Emperor. Rudolph II had yet to prove himself "in any Marshall causes" and was a political pawn of the Pope and King of Spain; he did not believe that Rudolph would ever recover any territory that he had already lost to the Turks, a large part of the Kingdom of Hungary. Most of the German soldiers Tyllney considered "base minded" and "of no accompt at all"; only the Hungarians were equal to the Turks. The people, in a typical sixteenth-century character sketch, were largely considered to be drunkards. Switzerland, Denmark, Poland, and Hungary are described in this book as bordering countries. He devotes most space to Switzerland, considered important because from it came the only mercenary soldiers of the time. The Swiss Cantons were allied to each other by special leagues, which Tyllney carefully reports, yet they were divided on the issue of religion, some of the Cantons practicing the "reformed religion."

This was important diplomatic information in view of the fact that the Swiss had in the recent past been employed in the service of the Pope and were tied by special treaties to the Emperor.

Spain was the country that Tyllney feared most, and with good reason. Not only did her dominions in Europe include the Kingdom of Naples in Italy and the Netherlands, but Spanish influence with the Pope and with the Emperor of Germany made her the most powerful and influential country in Europe. Her territories in the New World, commonly called "Peru" as Tyllney points out, were larger than those in Europe, bringing in a half-million a year in taxes. Further, her recent conquest of Portugal brought with it all of the Portuguese dominions in Arabia, Ethiopia, and India. As Tyllney counted it, Spain's navy was greater than any two of the greatest princes in Christendom and the King's revenues were so large that he estimated them at twice the amount of any other Christian prince. The people of Spain, whom Tyllney considered insolent, but not so "light conceited" as the French, were apt enough for military service but they were not all equally devoted to the King. Nevertheless, according to Tyllney's intelligence, the King had in a recent muster registered some 300,000 able-bodied men without much effort in Spain alone. Further, since King Ferdinand had been invested with the administration of the three orders of religious knights—Alcantara, Calatrava, and St. James—the Spanish monarchs' military power became undisputed; the nobility were kept well in line both by rich advancements from the King and by the Court of Inquisition. And lastly, the King was allied with the Pope and the princes of Italy and could count on mercenaries from Germany, Switzerland, and the Hanseatic League. Tyllney never quite forgot the attempted invasion of England, engineered by Pope Sixtus IV and Phillip II, and still regarded another invasion as a possibility. He described King Phillip II as old and impotent, "of Complexion flegmatike, which maketh hime the more patient and helpeth him to disemble the better and can take thereby his best opportunities for Revenge." This section, included in F1, was written before the King's death in 1598 and was dropped from F2. Tyllney also considered making a case for Elizabeth's title to Castile but abandoned that in F2 as well.

The Netherlands was of interest for two chief reasons. Foremost, it was an immediate drain on Spain's economy and thus a means of limiting her power. Tyllney estimated that Phillip II's wars in the Low Countries cost him "a hundred years Purchas at the lest." The interest on the King's debts alone consumed most of his ordinary revenues, estimated at nine million a year. As a result, for extraordinary enterprises, such as another invasion of England, he would have to raise the money by extraordinary means. Tyllney was also interested in the English claim to the title of Hainaut, derived through the marriage of Phillipa of Hainaut to Edward III of England. Apparently Tyllney felt that this was, if not the strongest, at least the most practical English claim to Continental territory, for he takes the matter up twice in the manuscript, once in his description of The Netherlands and again in the chronology of England.

As bordering countries Scotland and Ireland were diplomatically important to England, although less pleasing for Tyllney to write about. He makes no attempt to present these countries with distinguished histories as he does for England and the Continental countries. Scotland is treated with characteristic sixteenth-century English disdain. Its ancient name, Albania, Tyllney records, was derived from Albanact, a younger son of Brute, suggesting that the country was, in the contemporary phrase, a younger brother's portion. The country was so naturally fortified that Tyllney concluded "there could never be any thorough conquest made of the same by invasion." He felt compelled to slight the Scots pride in this knowledge by suggesting that it was the poverty of the country, not the strength of its fortifications or the valor of its people, that kept it safe from invasion. He notes that the King's estate was one of the weakest in Europe and that he was also one of the poorest monarchs whose revenues amounted to no more than £50,000 a year. The people are described as wild and unmannered, always ready to rebel, yet well prepared to defend the country from invasion. Tyllney made some serious allegations about the behavior of Lennox and Arran, who he suggests falsified their faith, during the intrigues surrounding the expulsion of Mary Queen of Scots. He thoroughly revised this section for F2, toning down the allegations to avoid offending the Scottish King James.

Tyllney's treatment of the Irish, as might be expected, is wholly contemptuous. The country was populated by "witty, vnfaithful, and subtill people full of witcheries and sorceries more to be doubted in peace then in open warres." They were fierce warriors but badly armed, whose chief strategy was to draw mounted knights into woods and bogs where they would be at a disadvantage. In their continual attempt to expel the English, the Irish had managed to restrict English control to the pale: the counties of Meath, Kildare, Louth, Wexford, and some part of Kingsland. Tyllney is never less than hostile towards the Irish who, as he states, under Queen Elizabeth's "peaciable regiment . . . haue nothinge swarved from their former disloyalties and accustomed rebellions."

Part of the attraction of writing about Italy was its culture and its massive influence on contemporary European institutions. Tyllney could not resist a chapter on Roman Law, an influence on virtually all of the legal institutions of Europe. Neither could he resist a description of the government and institutions of the Roman

Empire. Even the chronology for the books is historical, ending with Leo Constantine; it continues with Charlemagne in the book on Germany to focus on the continuity of the Holy Roman Empire. But Tyllney's main motive was to treat the three important powers in Italy—the Papacy, the Kingdom of Naples, and the Seigniory of Venice. He provides a historical discussion of the accumulation of temporal power by the Popes and investigates their responsibility for the politico-religious unrest in Europe at the time. Further, he is careful to record the influence in Italy of the Spanish King, who controlled Naples and, by virtue of his alliance with the Pope, was often at cross purposes with the Seigniory of Venice.

III

Certain aspects of Tyllney's manuscripts will be of value to scholars in a variety of fields, but the work is so wide-ranging that much of the material will not be of sufficient interest to any one of them. For the history of cartography, the manuscripts contain four unique copies of Peter Overadt's maps of *Italy, France, Germany,* and *Spain* (1598), and one of only two known copies of van den Keere's *Hybernia* (1591) and *Angliae Regnum* (ca. 1600). For the history of engraving, hundreds of portraits of the ecclesiastical and temporal princes of Europe, including three hitherto unknown copies of Benjamin Wright's portrait of King James I, are preserved. The value of the manuscripts for the heraldic historian and genealogist is obvious. They contain literally thousands of the names of the chief families of Europe and their coats of arms along with the genealogies of hundreds of the chief peers. Thomas Willement (1786–1871), heraldic artist to George IV and author of a number of works on heraldry and genealogy, used F1 as a working record of the heraldry and genealogy of England, adding 572 coats of arms and notes himself.

The work is less valuable to political than to social historians. For the latter, at least, it is interesting as an early attempt to organize intelligence information. But the very objectivity for which Tyllney strives in his work—selecting his information carefully, checking it and bringing it in accord with other standard sources, organizing it into a digest—the very qualities which distinguish it from the copious and amorphous products of the Renaissance, are, from our point of view in the twentieth century, its chief defects. We know the great bulk of information he includes from other sources and his studied objectivity prevents us from seeing his biases. When themes emerge—the Spanish domination of European politics or England's claim to foreign territory—they do so less from a conscious attempt to present an individual point of view than from acceptable English attitudes of the 1590s. Even the detailed character sketches of Rudolph II and Phillip II, for all their liveliness and interest, mainly reveal that Tyllney, like most Englishmen of his generation, never quite got over his fear and mistrust of the Spanish. The "Topographical Descriptions" serves political historians in the twentieth century much in the way it was intended to serve Elizabeth I and James I: it is a digest of diplomatic information, the bulk of which, with considerable effort and time, they could extract themselves from a myriad of manuscript and printed sources.

Despite its reliance on developing modern methods of scholarship and organization, Tyllney's work is not a history or even a diplomatic manual in the modern sense. It is a fossil, a record of a stillborn attempt to embody intelligence information in a rigid form. It represents, perhaps, the highest state of the art achievable by an individual on his own. Diplomatic intelligence in the modern world has by its very nature a short life span. It cannot be fixed in the form of a reference book. This fact, however, is not self-evident; it had to be learned in experience, and probably Tyllney himself began to recognize it after his third revision. But if its value as a new source for political historians is limited, its value to historians of dramatic censorship is increased. For, in the absence of much detailed evidence of Tyllney's procedure in censoring the drama, this work becomes the standard by which we measure not only the facts which he had at his disposal but also his political values and ideas. And since these values and ideas are so distinctly main line, the kind that the government itself might have pronounced in the 1590s, the work provides us with an important insight into the general quality of censorship exercised in the late Elizabethan drama.

Tyllney's appointment as the first official censor of plays in England by special commission in 1581 provided him with the extraordinary power to examine, alter, and allow or suppress every play written for public performance anywhere in the realm. To fortify his authority he was empowered to imprison for indefinite periods, without bail, anyone who violated his censures. Probably no single individual not directly connected with the theater industry itself has had so great an influence on the drama that has come down to us from that period. Unfortunately, we know less than we might wish about Tyllney's procedures in censoring the drama, but there is enough information about the conduct of the Masters of the Revels in this period to make some generalizations. G. E. Bentley, based on his study of surviving censorship documents, provides a list of the five categories of material which the censors attempted to suppress: (1) critical comments on the policy or conduct of the government; (2) satire of influential individuals; (3) unfavorable presentation of friendly foreign powers; (4) comment on religious controversies; and (5) after 1606, profanity.[19] We know that the London City Corporation exercised its power to jail actors who put on a play that Tyllney "did vtterly mislike."[20] On one occasion he managed to suppress a play that might have provoked civil unrest. The play was *The Book of Sir Thomas More,* three pages of which were possibly written by Shakespeare.[21] Tyllney heavily censored the play for its oblique references to an inflammatory topical issue, the anti-alien sentiments of the late 1580s and early 1590s.[22] As a result it was never produced.

The play deals, in part, with More's efforts to quell the anti-alien riots of May 1517. Practically all of the first scene, which shows the outrages committed by privileged foreigners against Londoners, was marked for omission. But there were other objections as well. Two passages in the third scene, in which the Privy Council discusses grievances against foreigners and the scene in which Bishop Fisher and More hesitate to sign articles submitted to the Council by the King were found objectionable. The latter scene is innocuous enough; not even the nature of the articles is made clear. But the suggestion that the Privy Council might hesitate in the slightest to conform to the sovereign's wishes was enough to suppress it. Tyllney also wanted "Lombard" sustituted for "ffrenchmen" and "straunger." Lombardy was under the control of Spain at this time and the English were allied with France and with the revolted provinces in the Netherlands against Spain. Compliance with Tyllney's directions for alteration would have involved rewriting a quarter of the play, which the dramatists apparently felt was too large a project to undertake.

T. W. Baldwin once suggested that the material in the "Topographical Descriptions" would settle once and for all the question of politically sensitive material on the Elizabethan stage.[23] While this is a useful generalization, it is one which promises more concrete information than the work is capable of delivering. There are no references to plays nor any outright indication of how Tyllney might have censored them. But the work includes information that relates to virtually all of the issues of censorship in the period. We know, for example, that in 1589 a joint censorship board was proposed which included a nominee of the Lord Mayor of London to represent the city's interest, a nominee of the Archbishop of Canterbury to represent the church's interest, and Tyllney, who represented the government. No record of their activities survives, and Chambers supposed that Tyllney managed to divest himself of their help.[24] But in the dedication to the "Topographical Descriptions" Tyllney excludes the subject of religious controversy. Quite clearly, he had no wish to pronounce officially on religious subjects, suggesting that Tyllney may have indeed relied on the advice of this board in religious matters. We know also that Shakespeare's characterization of Oldcastle, executed as a Lollard in 1417, was offensive to Protestant sensibilities in the late sixteenth century, and he changed the name of the character to Falstaff.[25] Tyllney includes notes on both families along with their coats of arms in the "Topographical Descriptions" (F2, ff. 328r, 333v), but, because he refused to treat sensitive religious issues, does not mention Oldcastle's execution or the reason for it. The omission suggests, perhaps, why the character was approved in the preliminary censorship. These few examples may suffice to suggest the relevance of this work to discussions of censorship in the period. For the historical backgrounds, the geography, the economics, politics, and even many of the characters that appear in the drama of the age are included in some form in Tyllney's work. The "Topographical Descriptions," then, reveals the extent of Tyllney's research, but it is not a work which clearly indicates the uses he made of it.

Tyllney's reading and research for the "Topographical Descriptions," stretching over most of his public career, put at his disposal more specific information than almost anyone at the Tudor court, which is, no doubt, why he undertook the project. And, while the work seems never to have been presented to the sovereign, it lay literally at Tyllney's fingertips in its completed form until his death in 1610. This fact alone, as Baldwin has suggested, is sufficient to indicate that not much would have passed Tyllney's censorship disguised as history or myth which might have obliquely applied in unfavorable ways to contemporary politics in England. Indeed, with respect to the first three of Bentley's categories of material which the censors attempted to eliminate from the drama—comments on the policy or conduct of the government, satire of influential individuals, and unfavorable presentations of friendly foreign powers—Tyllney was in a better position than most to judge what was or was not innocuous enough for public consumption. Certainly, any scholar hoping to discuss political censorship in England during this period will wish to consult the work.

IV
Sources and Influences

I

LIKE MOST OF HIS Renaissance contemporaries Tyllney relied heavily on sources. The "Topographical Descriptions" is a compilation, as Tyllney points out in his dedication, made up, for the historical material, from the "homeborne Writters (for Matters by paste) Written off ther own naturall Cuntries" and, for the contemporary material, from his "own Trauaill, and by Relation off suche, as had best Means to know the trueth." He reported only that which in his "own Concepte, Carried greatest reason, and likelihood off troth" before he felt that it was ready to be presented to King James who, as Tyllney suggests, did not have the "leysore for euerie cause, to ouerturne so many great Vollumes." It was a work of critical scholarship; Tyllney himself overturned the great volumes for a period of many years. He claims in the dedication to have been taking notes since his days as a young courtier. Some of the sources he employed substantiate the claim; but he had probably not taken them with the view of writing this work. All courtiers collected information of this kind simply as a means of participating knowledgeably in conversation at court. Tyllney's own notes do not survive, but the collections made by Sir Francis Bacon when he was a young courtier are representative of this kind of material.[1] By the time he began in earnest to write the "Topographical Descriptions" in the late 1590s, then, Tyllney had been collecting material, using the method that Davison recommends in his list of instructions—from published works, from private manuscripts, from confidential government documents, from personal observation, and from reports—for roughly thirty years. Insofar as the resulting work is a woven mesh of all these sources there is little to distinguish the "Topographical Descriptions" from its medieval predecessors. But insofar as Tyllney has diligently surveyed all of the available material, chosen it on critical principles, critically compared it, and reported only that which seemed true on these critical principles, his work is a genuine product of the Renaissance.

Regrettably, Tyllney does not often identify his sources. Usually his critical evaluation is expressed in a formula, such as "by some opinions . . . but by others," "as some do suppose," or "in some mens opinions." Identifying his sources, then, is limited primarily to observing parallels. In many instances, when Tyllney's wording is close to the wording of a source, clear-cut cases can be made; in others, when the text is such a pastiche of printed, manuscript, and verbal sources, the cases lend themselves more to speculation than to documentation.

The sources for the Continental books suggest that Tyllney had been collecting notes that were to be incorporated into his descriptions as early as his young courtier period. For some of the information included in his book on the Netherlands it is possible that Tyllney consulted a source as late as Jean Francois Le Petit's *La Grande Chronique, anciene et moderne* (Dordrecth, 1601), but it is certain that the mainstay of his description was Lodovico Guicciardini's *Descrittione di tutti i paesi bassi* (Anvers, 1567). Tyllney probably took notes from Guicciardini's Italian edition, the acknowledged standard work in the field, when he was a courtier. When he finally did write the book, however, he turned to Thomas Dannett's condensed translation.[2] He has relied so heavily on Dannett that it is possible to go through that work page for page picking out similar information down to the spelling of the place names. And since Dannett's translation is a condensed version, it is possible to distinguish where Tyllney follows him and where he follows the original Italian. Guicciardini, for example, gives a detailed topographical description of the town of Harlingen, which Dannet condenses.[3] Tyllney follows Dannett here, adding only that the garrison manning the town was Spanish—information that he probably derived from an English intelligence report. Much on this model does Tyllney emend or supplement the information he derived from his main sources in all of the books of the manuscript. The number of walled towns, the distances between cities, and other details are based either on manuscript sources or intelligence reports. The lists of the principal families were culled from Dannett and, perhaps, from Le Petit. For the coats of arms he relied in all cases, as he mentions in the dedication, on information that "came to hand"; some of it was derived from printed books but much of it, I suspect, came from private manuscripts or from reports. The genealogical information came primarily from Dannett and possibly some (that for the families of Gelders and Holland) from Le Petit. But all of these genealogies were checked against Guicciardini and against Elias Reusner's *ΒΑΣΙΛΙΚΩΝ* (Frankfurt, 1592), one of the few sources that Tyllney does cite.

For the genealogy of Phillipa of Hainaut, Tyllney went to Dannett, Guicciardini, Reusner, and other sources. The issue at stake was the English claim to the titles through Phillipa, wife of Edward III of England. Tyllney interprets the fact that "Reissnerus" makes her a younger daughter of Duke William IV and Guicciardini omits mention of her at all as an attempt to obscure the English claim to the titles and a defence of the Austrian right. In cases such as this, where he feels that a legitimate English claim exists, Tyllney was motivated to check as many sources as he could find. But even for the less controversial cases he often refers to more than one source.

The book on Germany contains material that dates from Tyllney's courtier period also. The mainstay of these early notes was Sebastian Münster's *Cosmographiae Universalis* (Frankfurt, 1554). The general description of the country, its boundaries, rivers, and government, as well as the genealogies and chronology are derived initially from Münster. All of the information, however, is corrected by other sources. The genealogies were corrected with Reusner's *ΒΑΣΙΛΙΚΩΝ*, and Wolfgang Lazius's *Geneologiam Austriacam* (Basil, 1564); the chronology is supplemented with another source, possibly Pedro Mexia's *Historia imperial y Cesarea* (Seville, 1547);[4] and the topographical information is supplemented by Lazius's *Chorographia Austriae* (Basil, 1558) and William Fiston's *The Estate of the Germaine Empier* (London, 1595). From Fiston Tyllney derived his accounts of the number of horse and foot soldiers that the nobility and clergy furnished in service against the Turk. Tyllney's accounts are more detailed, however, providing in addition the amount of money paid in lieu of service. This information is based either on his own calculations of the general assessment made at the Diet of Worms or on a confidential government document.

For his account of France Tyllney consulted Francois de Belleforest's *L'Histoire Universelle* (Paris, 1570) and *La Cosmographie* (Paris, 1575), and uses information for his general sections on the country, government, and for some of the topographical information. Almost all of the topographical information, however, is updated with John

Eliot's *The Survey or Topographical Description of France* (London, 1592). Tyllney's discussion of the revenue of the crown and the Chamber of Accounts and Court of Aids was probably derived from a goverment document. Dallington later provided similar information in his *View of France*; while Tyllney's tallies do not agree with Dallington's there are enough similarities to suggest a common source.[5] Perhaps I.R.'s translation of Botero's *The World* (London, 1601) provided the information for Tyllney's discussion of the administration of the country; if so, it was corrected with other documents, for the tallies do not agree on the expenses for the hired army. E.A.'s translation of La Noue's *Politike and Militarie Discourses* (London, 1587) provides the proposal for revamping the pay scale of the army.

The information for the description of Spain was derived from several sources. Theordore Turquet de Mayerne's *Somaire Description de la France, Allgemine, Italia, and Espana* (Paris, 1592) and Louis Mayerne Turquet's *Historia generale d'Espagne* (Paris, 1587) provide a good amount of topographical and genealogical information along with a description of Spain's three orders of knights. He probably read Conestaggio's *History of the Vniting of the Kingdome of Spain and Portugal* in E. Blount's translation (London, 1600), although there are no distinct verbal echoes in Tyllney's text. Pedro de Medina's *Grandezas y cosa memorable de Espana* (Sevill, 1548) provided a description of the rivers and the tables of mileages as well as a list of the bishops and peers and a full account of the succession of the kings of Spain. Tyllney would have found this work recommended by one of his sources, Ortelius, who supplied much of the information for the notes that are added to the margins of Fl.[6] Nevertheless, for the worth of Spanish peers and bishops and for the musters of able-bodied men in Spain Tyllney turned to confidential government documents.[7]

Tyllney may have been taking notes on Italy early in his career but he was still collecting them as late as 1600 and this seems to be the last of the books to have been completed. William Thomas's *History of Italy* (London, 1561) provided some of the notes for the general sections, the Roman chronology, the description of the city of Rome, and perhaps also the chronology of Popes. Nevertheless, all of this information was supplemented to the point where verbal parallels are obscured. The various descriptions of ancient Italy are in part derived from Ortelius and perhaps also from Leandro Alberti, *Descrittione di tutta Italia* (Bologna, 1550). Many of the comments on Italian history were probably derived from Francisco Guicciardini's *History*, tr. Geffray Fenton (London, 1599), and Machiavelli's *Florentine History*, tr. T.B. (London, 1595). Turquet's *Somaire Description* provided some of the topographical information, as did "Volaterranus."[8] The chronology was supplemented probably by Mexia's *Imperial History* and the account of Venice by Lewis Leuknor's translation of Contarini's *Commonwealth and Government of Venice* (London, 1595.)

The variety of sources and analogues that can be suggested for the Continental books and to a certain extent documented through verbal parallels and through works that Tyllney mentions indicates that these books were the first that he "trauailed" in. The sources also show that these early notes from Guicciardini, Thomas, Turquet, Münster, and Belleforest, all available by 1570, were substantially supplemented with sources not available until the 1590s. These later sources, Dannet (1593), Fiston (1595), Elliot (1592), and Leuknor (1595), some of which provide the bulk of information included in these books, indicate that Tyllney had not conceived of the work in its present form until the 1590s. The books on the British Isles contain information which could reasonably have been collected in the late 1570s but the heavy reliance on Camden indicates that the books could not have been written before 1586 and were probably written along with the rest in the late 1590s.

In his book on England Tyllney mentions several sources: Polydore Vergil, Elias Reusner, Claudius Ptolemy, Julius Caesar, and Guicciardini.[9] And while he is indebted to Holinshed, Harrison, Stowe, Giraldus, Ralph Brooke, and Powel's edition of Caradoc's *History of Cambria* for material, [10] the mainstay of his description was Camden's *Britannia*. Most of the topographical information down to the details of the Saxon script for some of the place names in medieval England are derived from Camden; much of the information that he quotes from Caesar and Ptolemy was also included in *Britannia*. The details on the number of market towns, forests, parks, and the mileages around the border of the shires comes from the table included in the catalogue at the beginning of Christopher Saxton's *An Atlas of England and Wales* (1579) and from the pack of geographical playing cards that are used to illustrate the margins of F1 in this book,[11] although the omission of some of the mileages suggests that Tyllney checked these with other sources. For his chapter on the division of the people in the English commonwealth he turned to Camden's "Ordines Angliae" in *Britannia* and to Harrison. He was probably familiar with Sir Thomas Smith's account as well, which in part duplicates Harrison's discussion, but it is clear that the details are derived from Harrison. Smith had probably seen Harrison's manuscript in 1577 and borrowed from it for his own *De Republica Anglorum* (London, 1583). When Harrison revised his manuscript for the 1587 edition of the *Description* he borrowed some of Smith's improvements on his original essay and Tyllney follows Harrison closely enough to confirm him as the source.[12] The same cross-borrowing between Smith and Harrison occurs in their account of the English parliament and Tyllney, in his chapter on the

Public Government of England, again relies on Harrison. Other scattered pieces of information such as the number of burgesses each town sent to parliament and the amount of money each bishopric sent to Rome as an alienation came from Harrison too. But for the valuations and tenths of bishoprics, which was listed in Harrison, he turned to a confidential government document.[13] He did the same for the court budgets and for his table of the inventory of the Royal Navy. For the description of the 1588 Victory Procession celebrating the defeat of the Armada, which set out the precedence of the English nobility, he relied on a manuscript description, possibly from the College of Heralds.[14]

It is clear that Tyllney did not have access to John Leland's notes. Harrison had confused and conflated Leland's account of salt works at Droitwich in Worcester and at Nantwich in Cheshire and Tyllney follows Harrison. He also follows Camden's account of the town of Plymouth verbatim (allowing for translation from the Latin), which Camden derived from Leland. Virtually all of the genealogical and peerage information is derived from Camden and from Ralph Brooke. He selects what he believes to be the best case from their arguments and in instances where conflicting evidence is strong he reports both opinions, albeit without mentioning either by name. He had access to a private manuscript for the coats of arms and notes on the chief families: Huntington MS. EL 318 (ca. 1605–12) is written on the same paper as both of Tyllney's manuscripts, contains similar, although not identical, notes, and contains 544 emblazoned coats of arms. It is possible that this manuscript derives from the same archetype that Tyllney employed.

Hector Boece's Description of Scotland, translated by Harrison and included in Holinshed's *Chronicles,* provided Tyllney with much of his information for that book. He seems to have turned to Joannes (Scotus) Major's *Historia*

Maioris Britanniae (Paris, 1521) for the general description of the country and for the rivers. The genealogical information is supplemented by Camden. Perhaps the account of the laws and government are derived from John Leslie (Bishop of Ross), *De origine, moribus, et rebus gestis Scotorum* (Rome, 1578). The chronology derives mainly from Holinshed's compilation but some of the details may have been taken from Leslie or Buchannan's *Rerum Scoticarum Historis* (Edinburgh, 1582).

Several readily available sources provided Tyllney with the material for his description of Ireland. John Hooker's compilation of the "Conquest of Ireland" and the "Chronicles" and Richard Stanihurst's translation of Giraldus Cambrensis (Archdeacon of St. David's), *Description and First Inhabitation of Ireland* were included in Holinshed's *Chronicles* and other information was printed in Camden's *Britannia.* Tyllney's account is corrected by reports, no doubt from courtiers involved in putting down Tyrone's rebellion. These reports are used to correct mainly the genealogical sections. The description of the Isles of Man, Jersey, Guernsey, and Wight which are included in this book were derived from Camden.

II

Tyllney was indebted for his method of scholarship to the sources he employed. Not only his organization but his critical comparison of sources and his treatment of history are all influenced by developments in sixteenth-century scholarship. This developing tradition is represented in the second half of the century by men like Harrison and Camden.

Harrison's *Description of England* was a transitional work. It was not a series of arbitrarily selected essays but it was loosely enough organized to encourage speculation from modern scholars on its coherence; Harrison produced the work from the "crumbs," as he calls them, that fell out of his *magnum opus,* "The Chronology," a work that never reached publication stage. He reports the familiar legends of Albion, the tales of giants, which he felt were not "mere fable to delight men's ears," gives accounts of ancient religions, the rivers of England with their tides, describes London Bridge and the 3,000 watermen who make their living on the Thames, the fruitfulness of the soil and wholesomeness of the air. Harrison went on to endear himself to posterity by giving a first-hand account of the daily life of the Englishman in the great age of Elizabeth, although his first book of the *Description* does not appear on the surface to be much different from its medieval predecessors. But if the structure of his description was transitional from the medieval *summa* to the highly organized work of Camden, its scholarship was already modern, his credulousness notwithstanding. His method was firmly grounded in the developing tradition of the scholar-antiquarians.

John Leland, the first of the great antiquarians of the early sixteenth century in England, made an empirical attempt to survey the country, a project which entangled him in such a mass of first-hand observations that he failed to produce a work on the subject. His notes, however, were widely circulated and provided later topographers and antiquarians, such as Harrison and Camden, with the bulk of material that is included in their works.[15] Harrison critically reviewed Leland's notes and checked out what seemed to him to be suspicious. He read earlier accounts, sent letters to respondents throughout England, and talked with people who might be expected to have accurate information. He was committed to avoiding the errors of his predecessors and was critical in his selection material: "I marked in what things the talkers did agree, and wherein they impugned each other, choosing in the end the former, and reiectinge the latter, as one desirous to set foorthe the truth absolutelie, or such things indeed as were most likely to be true."[16]

William Lambard claimed that a complete description of Britain was beyond the powers of a single man.[17] This was true enough within the antiquarian tradition which relied solely on empirical observation and sought to record everything. But before the end of the century Camden accomplished the task. *Britannia,* originally an attempt to use archaeological evidence to elucidate the Roman names of the island, first appeared as a small quarto in 1586 but grew in successive stages to include vast amounts of topographical, historical, and genealogical information not only on England, but on Scotland, Ireland, and the outlying islands as well.[18] The work introduced Continental methods of critical scholarship into England and earned for its author the title of the British Strabo. Camden's success was due to the critical perspective that he brought to the task. Empirical information was only one of many sources of evidence; like Harrison, Camden relied on earlier sources, chiefly Leland's notes, on discussions, and on respondents. But in contrast to Harrison, he does not include information simply because it was judged to be true on critical principles; Camden only includes information that relates to the main purpose of the work: to elucidate England's present by critically framing its past. This governing idea, under which all of the particular information is subsumed, provided Camden's *Britannia* with a unity which was lacking in English works of this type and suggested an organization. In *Britannia,* England was subdivided into the seventeen areas inhabited by the ancient British tribes and then further, if inconsistently, divided into the existing sixteenth-century shires. Within each of the sections on the shires, Camden provided general information on the antiquities, laws, government, political divisions, topographical descriptions of the towns, and a genealogy of the peers associated with the area. What he lost in linear consistency he gained in intelligibility, for he was able to treat the most diverse subjects, all of which were unified by their relationship to the central theme. That theme was the critical historical perspective that elucidated England's character or "estate."

Tyllney's "Topographical Descriptions" is a product of the developing tradition of critical scholarship in the sixteenth century. Truth for Tyllney meant the same that it did for Harrison, and their method of discovering it was identical—the critical comparison of sources from reading, discussion, and observation. Tyllney reports all of the mythological founders of the European countries. In England, for example, Brute, Samothes, and Mulmutius the lawgiver are all included in the general description of the country; yet, Tyllney is critical in writing about them, prefacing his account with "those that believe there was such a man" or "by the report of some writers." When he comes to what he considers to be the more strictly factual sections, the chronologies for example, he rejects them and excuses their omission on the ground that he lacks concrete evidence. The English chronology begins with Cassivelan (fl. 54 B.C.) because it is documented by "good report." King Arthur is also included in the chronology, but not the Arthur of Geoffrey of Monmouth who conquered all of Europe. Rather he is the Arthur of critical scholars like Sir Thomas Elyot and Sir Francis Bacon, who could write as late as 1622 about "that ancient worthy King of the Britains; in whose Acts there is truth enough to make him famous, besides that which is Fabulous."[19] Here as elsewhere it is the existence of archaeological evidence and critical arguments about it or the agreement of good sources that induces Tyllney to accept information. But the "Topographical Descriptions" derives its coherence not from its critically evaluated particular information but rather, like the *Britannia,* from the critical historical perspective that is brought to bear on the governing theme of the work—the elucidation of the "estate" of Europe—and the treatment of topics relevant to that theme. And if it can be said of Harrison that he crystallized the great age of Elizabeth in domestic detail, it might as well be said of Tyllney that he crystallized Europe in the great age of Elizabeth in diplomatic detail.

V
Revisions

I

THE MANUSCRIPTS PROVIDE enough internal evidence to permit a reasonably accurate view of the composition process. By his own account in the dedication to King James, Tyllney was collecting notes since his early days as a courtier. We may roughly identify this as the period between 1568, when he dedicated his *Flower of Friendshippe* to Queen Elizabeth, and 1579, when he received his formal appointment as Master of the Revels. The sources for the "Topographical Descriptions" reveal that the notes Tyllney had been collecting over the years were substantially supplemented by printed works not available until the period 1589 to 1595. External evidence about Tyllney's worsening financial position and the stir at court over the reversion of the patent for the Mastership of the Revels in 1597 suggest that it was not until the latter part of the decade that Tyllney began in earnest to prepare a draft for the work.[1] Dated notes from Italy, which appears to have been the last book completed, show that material was still being collected as late as 1600. In his description of Lombardy, for example, it is recorded that the Castle of Saluz was exchanged by King Henry

IV of France with the Duke of Savoy in "1600," a date which occurs several other times in this book.

Spain, Germany, and the Netherlands were probably the first accounts to have been written. Tyllney's assessment of Phillip II (1527–1598), "olde and Impotent, vpon the pointe of 70 yeres of his age," indicates that this section was written in 1597. There were many additions and revisions in these books when F2 was written, suggesting that they all date from before Phillip's death in 1598. The latest datable event in the book on France is the reference to the peace treaty of Vervins between Henry IV and Phillip II which occurred on 2 May 1598. France seems to have been the fourth book to have been written. From the references to Tyrone's rebellion, it seems clear that the draft for Ireland was not completed until after 1598. In his book on England, Tyllney refers to Essex and Southampton as if they still held their dignities; Devereux was executed on 25 February 1601 and Wriothesley was confined to the Tower until his release by King James on 16 May 1603.[2] Of the main books of the manuscript, Spain, the Netherlands, and Germany all seem to have been written before 1598; France, along with England, Ireland, and Scotland, were written after 1598 and before 1601; Italy appears to have been the last book to be completed and was written between 1600 and 1601.

Since many notes were added to the margins of the texts of Spain, Germany, and the Netherlands, and a few to England, it appears that F1 was prepared in stages from the drafts as they were completed between 1597 and 1601. The manuscript was fully illustrated with maps, engravings, and coats of arms, indicating that at one time it was intended to be the presentation copy. Perhaps Elizabeth's unwillingness to settle the matter of the reversion of the Mastership of the Revels postponed plans for presentation, but the death of Phillip II would have rendered the book on Spain in this manuscript obsolete in any case. After the completion of F1, Tyllney collected more notes and added many of these to the margins of the text. The new information on Spain included lists of the nobility and their yearly worth and the deletion of the section on the assessment of Phillip II and a few other minor sections. Tyllney also added a section on the division of the people in Spain, incorporated the appendices—the musters and the form of address between the King and his parliament—into the text, and corrected the genealogies. The additions for Germany are topographical and genealogical, and the material added to the Netherlands is primarily genealogical. This note-taking and revision was completed before Queen Elizabeth died.

F2 itself was completed before Elizabeth's death on 24 March 1603. Tyllney refers to her in the text continually as if she were still alive and the chronology of England originally ended with a note on her reign. For the production of this manuscript a new set of maps and engravings was collected and a new set of coats of arms was painted in. F1 and drafts for the separate revisions served as the copy text. F2 scribes have unintentionally dropped lines when copying from F1 and while in many cases the additions and revisions are based on marginal notes included in F1, the wording of the F2 text and the marginal notes in F1 are different enough to suggest that Tyllney provided separate drafts of this material for the scribes to work from. The number of scribes employed in the production of F2 and the cancelled foliation suggest that the manuscript was prepared by scribes working simultaneously on different parts of the text. That both sets of foliation were completed before binding is evident from the fact that some of the numbers of both sets were partially cropped in the trimming process. The cancelled foliation agrees initially with the foliation of F1, but by the seventh book there is a sixty-one- to sixty-two-digit difference between the cancelled and revised numbers of F2. The scribes appear to have begun by copying the foliation of F1, but additions to the manuscript and the larger handwriting of F2's scribes eventually forced renumbering the leaves.

Tyllney never corrected the references to Essex and Southampton. But sometime shortly after Elizabeth's death he revised F2 for presentation to King James. He added Elizabeth's obituary to the chronology of England and provided a note on James's accession here and in the rewritten chronology for Scotland. He also altered the section of the chronology on Mary, Queen of Scots, corrected the text, and added a dedication to the King. Tyllney speaks of the King's "promise" in these additions, suggesting that they were made very early in the reign, probably before 21 May 1603, at which time Sir Lewis Leuknor was appointed Master of Ceremonies at James's court. Tyllney appears at this point to have abandoned work on the manuscript.

The evidence, then, suggests that the manuscript was prepared in four stages:

1. ca. 1568 – ca. 1600
   Notes (lost)
2. ca. 1597 – 25 February 1601
   Draft (lost); F1
3. 25 February 1601 – 24 March 1603
   Notes (margins of F1); Drafts for Revisions (lost); F2
4. 24 March 1603 – 21 May 1603
   Additions and Revisions (F2)

Despite Tyllney's efforts, even F2 is not a finished work. Details such as mileages, valuations of the bishoprics, notes to the coats of arms, and some of the coats of arms themselves were never inserted into the spaces that he left for them. We can only speculate on why he did not complete the work. Disappointment over his failure to get the promotion he wanted is probably the major reason. But the world that Tyllney flourished in was collapsing. He was himself by this time in his sixties; his wife died shortly after this disappointment; his financial position was worsening, and he was involved in suits to hold on to family land, unsuccessfully it appears; he was confronted by a competitor in the office that he had held for twenty-four years, whose income depended on Tyllney's death; but perhaps most disorienting of all, at least as far as his official work was concerned, was Queen Elizabeth's death. James's accession changed the face of European politics and the hierarchy of the English nobility and rendered the manuscript obsolete as a diplomatic tool. James embarked almost immediately on a policy of reconciliation with Spain. And while Tyllney's patronizing remarks about Scotland may have been overlooked, his entire attitude toward European politics, dominated by his focus on Spanish influence, would no longer serve.

II

F2, as the authorially supervised revision, has substantive authority; it must be emended, however, with the readings unintentionally omitted by the scribes from F1. Since F1 was prepared from Tyllney's draft and therefore on the average embodies more of Tyllney's accidentals than F2 which derives from F1 and revised drafts, it has accidental authority. A study of the extant examples of Tyllney's holograph documents confirms that on the average F1 is closer to Tyllney's known practice in accidentals.

Only a few pieces of Tyllney's holograph have been identified. We have his letter to Sir William More, 25 January [1594–95]; the comment on a petition by some creditors of the Revels Office to Lord Burghley, 1597; the famous censorship direction in *The Book of Sir Thomas More,* [ca. 1592–94]; the additions to F1, ca. 1597–1601; the additions to F2, 1601–1603; a page and a half of the Revels Account for 1585; and a number of signatures on various documents.[3] Since these specimens range over the period from 1585 to 1603 and are written under varying conditions, they are sufficient to provide a general idea of Tyllney's practice over the years. His individual habits in spelling, punctuation, construction, and orthography are not remarkably unusual for the period. But when these various aspects of his writing are considered in concert they provide a roughly accurate means of distinguishing his habits from the scribes.

The letter to More and the note to Burghley, because they are the longest continuous specimens of his hand in which he was at leisure to employ forms that he might normally use, are the most important documents for most of these tests. The remaining specimens are additions and are constrained by space limitations or, as in the case of the indexes to F2, by the formal requirements of the task. We can assume that he would abbreviate more readily, capitalize where the task demanded it, and use punctuation where he might not otherwise, and so these additions are used primarily for spelling tests.

Tyllney was fond of doubling certain letters, especially the *f, t,* and *l,* and less frequently the *o, p,* and *r:* (att, butt, nott, yett, greatt, wrott, inhabitantts, thwartts, partte, sett, lett, writtinge, reportt, shortt; off, yourselff, chyffly, thereoff, wheroff, hymselff, officers, cheiffe; willingly, severall, brawlles, Admirall, requitall, couller, reueall; verry, perrilles; appealed, vppon, oppinions; prooued). He favored *y* spellings (maye, chyffly [also chiffly], complayned, ayny, awaye, hym, wyntertyme, lycens, saythe, praye, layd, certayne, teyd, Agaynst, mayors, Spayne, Foyxe [also Foix], Lorayn, Brittayn). More often than not he deletes the silent *e* in compound words (therwth, theroff, wheroff, whervnto, wherfore) but he usually tacks on a silent *e* to *y* and *ing* endings (conseruinge, Compoundinge, Agreinge, readinge, praye, awaye, saye, saythe, thinke, neighbore, wyntertyme, writtinge, longe, Spayne, kinge, cheiffe). For plurals he most often favors *es* over *s* (brawlles, coppies, demandes, silkes, afterwardes, townes, but also: inhabittantts, Revells, Quens, officers). On occasion he uses *e* for *ee, ie,* or *i* (ded, frendship, Agreinge, but Admirall is consistently spelled with an *i*). He was always inclined to abbreviate y^{e}, w^{th}, y^{t}, w^{ch}, y^{ts}, m^{r}, S^{r}, $m^{ate(s)}$, S^{t}, y^{em}, and usually &, *L,* and y^{es}; y^{er} alternates throughout with *ther.*

Tyllney wrote mainly in italic, but the influence of some secretary forms can be seen in the letter to More and in some of the longer additions to F1, especially in the *ss* () and *st* (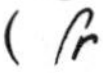) ligatures, in the terminal *t* (), and in some cases of the terminal *s* () and initial *f* (). The rest of his letter forms are clearly italic. He employed *v* for initial *v* or *u* and alternates between *v* and *u* for medials (receuid, ouer, seuerall, leaue, severall, Revells, services, friuilus, causes, shuld). He used the majuscule form for all initial letters except *k*; for this letter he habitually used the minuscule form even in the indexes to F2. In these indexes he also employed a majuscule *F* but in the letter to More, the only other occurrence of this letter in his holograph, he used *ff*. In the samples taken from the letter to More and the note to Burghley, Tyllney capitalized the following initials: *A* 15 of 41 times; *B* 2 of 21 times; *C* 21 of 28 times; *E* 6 of 6 times; *G* 3 of 8 times; *I* invariably; *L* 8 of 17 times; *R* 1 of 9 times; *S* 7 of 29 times; *T* 2 of 26 times; *V* 2 of 11 times; and *W* 7 of 38 times. He uses medial majuscules only twice.

Tyllney was not overly generous with punctuation. In the letter to More (670 words) he used twenty pieces of punctuation, an average of one in sixty-seven words; in the note to Burghley (109 words) he used three pieces, one in thirty-six words. He favored the virgule and used it in its single form eleven times and in its double form four times. The double virgule functions as a strong comma or as a full stop. The single virgule is the utilitarian mark; it functions as a weak or strong comma, or as a full stop. The comma, functioning in its modern sense, was used six times. The period was used once at the end of a passage as a full stop, but full stops occur in mid-line without any mark whatsoever.

Tyllney did not rely chiefly on punctuation to point his sentences. Rather he used it to break up the clauses in his long, loose, Latinate constructions. His sentences are sometimes whole paragraphs in which the main clause is often buried well within. He relies for intelligibility chiefly on the coordinating and subordinating conjunctions and on relative clauses. Short sentences are used to achieve a transition between paragraphs and, on some occasions, to relieve the monotony of the longer sentences. In general, paragraphing occurs for new topics. Because of the nature of the "Topographical Descriptions" this is the most natural, albeit the most mechanical, method of organization. In the letter to More, in which several subjects are discussed, there are no paragraphs at all. Despite the fact that it is sometimes difficult to determine where one of his sentences should end, the heavy use of conjunctions provides logical prominence for his main ideas, even when the relatives detract from it. In general, his construction habits are common for this period.

VI
Provenance

IF EITHER MANUSCRIPT was ever presented to the King it was lost before the Royal Library was deposited in the British Museum by George II in 1757, for it is not listed in the catalogue of the Old Royal and Kings collection.[1] If we assume, as seems most likely, that both manuscripts remained in Tyllney's possession, then three routes of descent are possible.

Tyllney stipulated in his will that his books were to be divided between the Reverends Michael Rabbett, Parson of Streatham, and Griffith Vaughan, Parson of Ashted.[2] Rabbett, one of the translators of the New Testament for the King James Bible, died in 1630 and ordered an inventory of his Latin, Greek, and Hebrew texts. They were to be stored until his grandchild should "prove a scholar"; if not, they were to be divided between his nephews, then studying at Cambridge. His audit does not seem to have survived. Vaughan, who made his will on 20 June 1610, ten days before Tyllney made his own, divided his books among his sons with the exception of two which were presented to his overseers, Parson Robert King of "Tileston in Chessire and John Reeve doctor of divinitie and Vicar of great Bookham." Possibly, one or both of the manuscripts were among the books divided between Rabbett and Vaughan and so passed down through their families.

Sir George Buc, Tyllney's successor in the Revels office, was an avid historian and antiquary.[3] It is altogether possible that Buc inherited the manuscripts with the office after Tyllney's death, since the information contained in them bore on his official duties as censor of plays. When Buc died a battery of suits were filed over the disposition of his estate. In a deposition taken in one of these suits, Francis Fowler reported that Buc's books were shared among a number of people and mentions "one fayre great Booke of Arms, iudged to be worth a greate Summ of money" which came into the possession of John Selden.[4] If this book was one of Tyllney's manuscripts it was among that part of Selden's library which was lost or misplaced before that collection was deposited in the Bodleian.[5]

The most likely route of descent was within the family itself. Edmond's executor, Thomas Tyllney, was to have the remainder of the estate after specific bequests were satisfied. It is likely that the manuscript came to Thomas and was passed down through the family. There is a note to the coat of arms for Palmer in the book on England in F2 in an eighteenth century hand: "from hence is descended ye Earle of Castlemayne 1661."[6] To the writer of this note, perhaps the owner for whom the manuscript was bound in its red morocco cover, the descent of the Earls of Castlemaine was of importance; this is significant since there are very few instances of later tampering with the text of F2. Roger Palmer was created Baron of Limrick and Earl of Castlemaine on 11 December 1661; when he died in 1705 his honors became extinct.[7] Richard Child was created Viscount Castlemaine on 24 April 1718 and married Dorothy Glynne, heiress of the Tyllney fortune and estates. Dorothy was a daughter of John Glynne of Henley Park, Somerset, and Dorothy, sister of Frederick Tyllney of Rotherwick. This branch of the family descended from William Tyllney of North Creek, Lincolnshire, third son of Sir Frederick Tyllney of Boston, and younger brother of Sir Phillip Tyllney of Boston (d. 1453), great-great-grandfather of Edmond Tyllney. By Act of Parliament on 24 May 1734 Dorothy's husband, Richard Child, who had been created Earl of Castlemaine on 11 June 1731, and his sons, assumed the name of Tyllney. It is possible that the manuscript either came into the Earl's possession as part of the estate, or was owned by another member of the family who traced this dignity associated with the Tyllney name. John Tyllney succeeded his father as Earl of Castlemaine, and when he died on 16 December 1784 the inheritance passed through general heirs eventually to the honorable William Pole-Tyllney-Long-Wellesley, fourth Earl of Mornington, who "pulled down the stately mansion at Wansted and Rotherwick, and dilapidated generally the vast estates of the families of Child and Tyllney."

There are no watermarks on the binder's leaves of F1. Di Ricci suggested that it was bound in its brown cover sometime in the early nineteenth century.[8] From the blind-stamped coat of arms (a saltire) in each corner of the cover, he also suggested that the manuscript belonged to the Dering family. I have not been able to confirm this. But sometime in the nineteenth century it almost certainly belonged to Thomas Willement (b. 1786; d. 10 March 1871), heraldic artist to George IV, artist in stained glass to Queen Victoria, Fellow of the Society of Antiquaries, and author of a number of heraldic and antiquarian works.[9] There are 572 additions to the coats of arms in the book on England which record creations of peers and their deaths between 1776 and 1782. While the handwriting varies drastically in some of these additions, I have determined from a comparison between these additions and the Willement manuscripts at the

Folger Shakespeare Library that they were all made by Willement at different times. He had, no doubt, collected the manuscript for his research and used it as a partial record of the heraldry of England.

I have not been able to trace the location of the manuscript after Willement's death in 1871. But in September 1924 it was sold by Maggs Brothers to the Folger Trust. Maggs, who had sold a number of Willement items to the Folger in 1923, followed up with another Willement piece in November 1924.[10] It is possible that the Tyllney manuscript came from the same source as the rest of these Willement pieces, but it was sold as an anonymous heraldic manuscript and so catalogued until my identification in August 1973. This manuscript remains in the Folger Shakespeare Library, Washington, D.C.

The Foley bookplate is tipped to the inside cover of F2. When the manuscript was acquired by that family is difficult to say. The Foley peerage dates from 1711, but the family had sufficient means and inclination to have collected a work such as this as early as the mid-seventeenth century and it could have been collected as late as the nineteenth century,[11] perhaps from the fourth Earl of Mornington in the process of "dilapidating" his family fortune. The manuscript was part of the Foley family library, one of the most distinguished collections of Elizabethan literature of its time, until its sale at Ruxley Lodge, Claygate, Surrey, on 27 October 1919. J. R. P. Lyell attended this sale and annotated his copy of the sale catalogue.[12] The Tyllney manuscript was bought by Quaritch Ltd. and sold immediately after the auction to an unknown party. In May 1955 the manuscript was sold by C. A. Stonehill, New Haven, to the University of Illinois Library at Urbana. The manuscript remains at the University in the Ernest Ingold Collection.

VII
Description of the Manuscripts

I. TITLES

(F1) [Tyllney, Edmond.] "THE Diſscriptions Regimentts and Pollicies as well Generall, as particularly of *Italy* | *France, Germanie, Spaine, England, & Scotland,* etc: by the ſeuerall particularities | wherof, The parfitt eſtate of eche one of them Maie generallie | be diſcouered." [1600–01.] *Di Ricci,* 1300.1 Folger Shakespeare Library MS., V.b. 182, Washington, D.C.[1]

(F2) Tyllney, Edmond. *"The Topographical deſcriptions Regimentes and Pollicies off Ittalie | France, Germanie: England, Spayne, Scotland and Ireland: | Wherby In ſom̃ ſorte the Particulare Estates off euerie one off | thos Contries maie be Diſcouered:"* [1601–03.] University of Illinois Library MS., uncat., Urbana, Illinois.

II. COLLATIONS

(F1) 373 leaves, nine folding maps. 2°: [5] 2 [1] 4–74, 76, 78–79, 38–42 [1] 43–78, 80–85, 90–126 [1] 130–134, 134–143 [1] 144–167 [1] 168–202 [1] 203–257, 259–277, 279–297, 299 [1] 300–304, 307–308, 310–322, 324–328, 330–331, 333–334, 337–348 [1] 349 ff.

(F2) 394 leaves, nine folding maps. 2°: [7] 1–50, 50–54, 56–86 [1] 87–136 [1] 137–185 [1] 186–211 [1] 212–228, 228–236, 236–246 [1] 247–342 [1] 344–366, 377–378, 377–378, 378–385 [1] 386, 388–398 ff. Cancelled foliation: ff. 1–63, 67–74 corresponds to 1–50, 50–54, 56–72; 81–118 corresponds to 93–130; 120–158 corresponds to 139–179; 160–177 corresponds to 188–205; 168–186 corresponds to 214–228; 228–231; 200–260 corresponds to 261–322; 255 corresponds to 346.

III. PAPER

(F1) Heavy weight, grained, buff paper, 41 × 26 cm. Ninety-eight leaves have printed rules for the purpose of emblazoning the coats of arms; the remaining leaves are ruled into single or double columns for the text. Watermarks are distributed as follows: ff. [i]–[iii], 43, 95–125, 145–165, 170–198, 203–251, 300–333, 341–348 are *Heawood,* 2091; ff. 4–67, 44–54 are *Heawood,* 2148; ff. 68–69 are *Heawood,* 2137; ff. 55–94 are similar to *Heawood,* 2135; ff. 199–200 are *Heawood,* 2146; ff. 41–42, 127–143, 166–169, 201–202, 252–299, 334–340 are *Heawood,* 2147; f. 349 [a crown atop a crest with a label below]; f. 126 is a lighter paper and bears no watermark. Four binder's leaves; no watermarks; end papers marbled.

(F2) Heavy weight, grained, buff paper, 39 × 26 cm.; f. 138 is untrimmed and f. 213 is partially trimmed at right. Forty-eight leaves have printed rules for the purpose of emblazoning the coats of arms; the remaining leaves are ruled into single or double columns for the text. Watermarks are distributed as follows: ff. [vi]–80, 85–130, 135–142, 147–179, 185–205, 210–240, 245–246, 257–280, 286–300, 341–343, 377, 384, 390–396 are *Heawood,* 2166; ff. 143–146, 248–256 are *Heawood,* 2156; ff. 281–285, 301–314 are *Heawood,* 2148; ff. 315–322 are *Heawood,* 2145; ff. 344–376, 385–389 are *Heawood,* 2137; ff. 81–84, 131–134, 180–184, 206–209, 241–244, 323–340, 378–383, 397–398 are *Heawood,* 2091. Sixteen binder's leaves; watermark: *Heawood,* 1795a (1676).

IV. BINDINGS

(F1) Late eighteenth- or early nineteenth-century brown calf. The cover, 42 × 26.3 cm., is blind stamped with a fusil (30 × 15 cm.) at center, the points of which terminate in fleurs-de-lis. Two double border rules form 2 cm. squares in each corner within which are coats of arms (a saltire). Edges trimmed.

(F2) Seventeenth-eighteenth century red morocco. The cover, 40 × 26.3 cm., is gilt stamped with a double border rule. The spine, seven ribs between eight panels, is gilt stamped with floral devices and the title: | TILLNEYS | HISTORY |. Edges trimmed and gilt.

V. MAPS

(F1) 1. | EVROPAE |, 331 × 470 mm. (right border cropped), n.d., unsigned. The map is a projection of Europe, North Africa, and the Middle East. An emblematic figure of Europa and a bull is located near the center of the left border and the title appears in free roman capitals below. The left and lower borders contain degrees of latitude and longitude. Unidentified.

2. | *Tabula Hydrographica ac Geographica* | [Italy], 387 × 525 mm. (torn at right border and top), n.d. [1590], Pet[rus Plancius]. In the upper right is a front aspect of Venice (72 × 95 mm.). [See *B.M. Maps,* VII, 1094.]

3. | GALLIA | Geographica Galliae descriptio . . . | auctore Petro Plancio | Ioannes Baptista Vrints excudit |

. . . | 1592 |, 398 × 485 mm. This map which is included in the 1606 edition of *Theatrum Orbis Terrarum* in the "Parergon" comes in two states; the first does not mention Vrients in the title block and the second is as above. [See, State no. 1: *B.M. Maps,* XI, 626; State no. 2: Koeman, III, p. 63, No. 150.]

4. | Deutschlanndt | GER: | MANI: | AE TY: | PVS. |, 370 × 480 mm., 1576, Franciscus Hogenberg. [See Koeman, III, p. 62, No. 147.]

5. | INFERIOR GERMANIA |, 388 × 497 mm. (cropped at left and right), 1593, Jodocus Hondius. The map is oriented west. [See *B.M. Maps,* X, 390.]

6. | REGNI | HISPANIAE POST | OMNIVM EDITIO: | NES LOCVPLTEISSI | MA DESCRIPTIO. |, 375 × 493 mm. (cropped at right border), n.d., unsigned [1570, Abraham Ortelius]. [See Koeman, III, p. 34, No. 7.]

7. | ANGLIA, | REGNUM | *Si quod aliud in* | *toto Oceano ditis:* | *simum et flo:* | *rentissimum.* |, 380 × 473 mm., n.d., unsigned [1602–03, Saxton-Ortelius]. The title is within a cartouche at the upper right; at left border, near center, within a cartouche, | *Christo:* | *phorus* | *Saxton* | *descri:* | *bebat.* | *1579.* |; above left are the arms of Elizabeth within the garter inscribed as usual; below right, within a cartouche, the "scala miliarum." [See Koeman, III, pp. 61–62, No. 143; and Shirley, p. 89, no. 258 and pl. 53.]

8. Fifty-two small maps of the shires of England and Wales (27 × 44 mm.) are tipped in the margins of the text of England from f. 211r to 250v. The maps have been cut from a pack of geographical playing cards: W[illiam] B[owes], 1590. [See S. Mann and D. Kingsley, "Playing Cards," *Map. Coll. Circle,* No. 87 (1972), pp. 4–5, pl. 1; and Skelton, pp. 16–18, pls. 4, 5.]

9. | SCO: | TIAE TA: | BVLA. |, 439 × 470 mm., n.d., unsigned [1573, Abraham Ortelius]. The map is oriented west. [See Koeman, III, p. 38, No. 1.]

10. | HYBER | NIAE | novissima descriptio | 1591 |, 336 × 509 mm., Pieter van den Keere. [See Hind, I, p. 206.]

(F2) 1. | EVROPAE |, 337 × 457 mm., n.d., unsigned [1570, Abraham Ortelius]. The title is in the upper left on a sarcophagus atop of which sits an emblematic figure of Europa and a bull; in the lower left there are three scales of miles: British, German, and Italian. [See Koeman, III, p. 34, No. 5.]

2. | ITALIA | totius Europae brachiũ, | *antiquitate praes tantissima,* | *sedes Pontificia* | *Peter Ouerradt imprimit Coloniae An.* 1598 |, 363 × 466 mm. (bottom border cropped). Below at center is a panel 123 × 110 mm. containing an emblematic engraving with a verse beginning | *Me beat ingenium, pietas ioca suada, sales que* |; in the upper right, within an oval border inscribed | CLEMENS VIII PAPA FLORENTINVS OPT. MAX. PONTIFEX ET PRINCEPS. MDXCVIII | is a portrait of the Pope with a caption | *Creatus 2 Februarij* | *Anno Salutis 1592* | *Aetatis. 54.* |. The engraving is after van de Passe; see Hollstein, XV, p. 227, No. 704. [See Streitberger, *Maps,* pp. 47–48.]

3. | GALLIA |, 367 × 463 mm. (bottom border cropped), n.d. [1598], in the lower right: | *Coloniae* | *formis Petri Ouerradt* |. In the lower left is a panel 125 × 111 mm. containing an emblematic engraving with a verse beginning | *Numina bina mihi celebrantur Pallas et Hermes* |; at the left border, near center, within an oval border inscribed | HENRICVS IIII. DEI GRATIA FRANCIAE, GALLIAE ET NAVARRAE REX CHRISTIANISS. | is a portrait of the king with a caption, | DV BON ROY | BON HENR. |. [See Streitberger, *Maps,* pp. 47–48.]

4. | GERMA- | NIA | TOTIVS EV- | ROPAE REG- | *num amplissimum ac* | florentissimum | *Sedes* | IMPERATORIA. | [device] | *Coloniae formulis Petri Ouerradij. 1598* |, 360 × 486 mm. Above the title is a cartouche with an inner border inscribed | IMPERIVM SINE FINE DEDI | within

which is a two-headed eagle; below right is a panel (123 × 111 mm.) containing an emblematic engraving with a verse beginning | *Hic Regina suas, Orbi Germania gazas* |; above left, within an oval border inscribed | INVICTISSIMVS RVDOLPHVS II. D. G. ROMAN IMPERATOR SEMPER AVGVSTVS | is a portrait of the Emperor with a caption | AD SIT |. [See Streitberger, *Maps,* pp. 47–48.]

5. | LEO | BELG | IC | V | S |, 360 × 440 mm., 1583, Michael Aitsinger. The title is above and left of center in free roman capitals; at the right border, above center, is a panel (230 × 84 mm.) containing a prose passage beginning | MICHAELIS | *Aitsingeri Austriaci ad Leonem* | *pro lectore introductio* |; the country is represented in the shape of a lion facing right. [See R. V. Tooley, "Leo Belgicus: An Illustrated list of variants," *Map. Coll. Circle,* No. 7 (1964).]

6. | HISPANIAE | REGNVM |, 360 × 482 mm., n.d. [1598], below right, within the border is the signature | *Coloniae formis Petri Ouerradt* |. The title is in the upper left; below right is a panel (125 × 111 mm.) containing an emblematic engraving with a verse beginning | *Regna tot una rego, quot cetera Numĩa getẽs,* |; at the right border, near center, within an oval border inscribed | PHILIPPVS D. G. HISPANIARVM, INDIARVM, NEAP. SICIL. HIEROSOL. ETC. REX CATHOLICVS | is a portrait of Philip II with a caption | DOMINVS MIHI | ADIVTOR |. [See Streitberger, *Maps,* pp. 49–50.]

7. | ANGLIAE | REGNVM |, 352 × 487 mm., n.d. [ca. 1600], Peter Kaerius [van den Keere]. The title is at the right border, near center; above the title is a panel (141 × 72 mm.) containing a catalogue of shires from Saxton's *Atlas* (1579) with an introduction beginning | CATALOGUS *Vrbium Episcopatuum Oppidorum mercato:* | *riarium Castrorum* |; at the left border, near center, | *Christo:* | *phorus* | *Saxton* | *descri:* | *bebat.* | *1579.* | *Petrus* | *Kaerius* | *caelavit.* | is inscribed within a cartouche; in the lower left, within

a cartouche, are two scales of miles: British and German. The descriptions of the British Museum's copy of this map in *Shirley*, pp. 80–81, No. 224, and *Skelton*, p. 135, are inaccurate. Shirley apparently follows Skelton in attributing the unusual spelling of Saxton's name (i.e., Saxston) in the 1660 edition to the 1600 edition also. [See Streitberger, *Maps*, pp. 49–51; the British Museum's copy, *Maps* C.2.cc.2 (17.), is not listed in the Catalogue.]

8. | SCO: | TIAE TA: | BVLA. |, 350 × 470 mm. [See (F1) Maps, Scotland.]

9. | ERYN. | HIBERNIAE, | BRITANNICAE | INSVLAE, NOVA | DESCRIPTIO. | Irelandt. |, 350 × 478 mm., n.d., unsigned [1573, Abraham Ortelius]. The title is within a cartouche in the upper right; the scale of miles is within a cartouche in the lower left; oriented west. [See Koeman, III, p. 38, No. 4.]

VI. ENGRAVINGS

(F1) Book I (Italy). Tipped to the back of the map are two (originally three) engraved portraits: *a.* Within an oval border inscribed | PHILIPVS II. CATHOLICVS. D. G. HISPANIARVM INDIARVMQ REX, DVX BRABANT, &c. AN. D. M.D.XCV | is a portrait of the king; 153 × 112 mm. (cut oval); unsigned. *b.* Within an oval border inscribed | ILLVSTRISSIMVS PASCHALIS CICONIA DVX VENETORVM, ANNO DOMINI MDXCVIII | is a portrait of the Duke; within the oval border and beneath the portrait is the motto | FORTITER ET | FIDELITER |; below is a Latin passage; 96 × 131 mm. (cut rectangular); monogram [Crispin van de Passe] [See Hollstein, XV, p. 227, no. 703.]. On f. 10v within an oval border inscribed | ss CLEMENS VIII. PAPA FLORENTINVS OPT. MAX. PONTIFEX ET PRINCEPS ANNO DNI. M.D.XCVI | is a portrait of the Pope; 108 × 83 mm. (cut oval); unsigned

[Crispin van de Passe] [See Hollstein, XV, p. 227, no. 704.]. On f. 33r within an oval border inscribed | PHILIPPVS II CATHOLICVS D. G. HISPANIARVM INDIARVMQVE REX POTENTISS. DVX BRABANTIAE | is a portrait of the king; within the oval border and beneath the portrait is the motto | NEC SPE NEC | METV |; 110 × 84 mm. (cut oval); n.d.; unsigned [Crispin van de Passe] [See Hollstein, XV, p. 269, no. 805.]. On f. 51v is another portrait of Paschalis Ciconia; 108 × 84 mm. (cut oval) [see above].

Book II (France). Tipped to the back of the map are two engraved portraits: *a.* A portrait of the King inscribed | HENRICVS .4. D. G. REX FRANCORVM | & NAVARRAE, AETATIS 42. ANNO. 1594 |; below is a passage in French; 154 × 92 mm. (cut rectangular); Jacob Grantsome [Similar to Hen. Goltzius; see Hollstein, VIII, p. 53.]. *b.* Within an oval border inscribed | CAROLVS *eius nominus* III. DEI GRATIA LOTHARINGIAE DVX. 1594 | is a portrait of the Duke; within the oval border and beneath the portrait is the motto | OPTANDA BONIS | PAX |; 143 × 112 mm. (cut oval); monogram [Crispin van de Passe] [See Hollstein, XV, p. 224, no. 649.].

Book III (Germany). Tipped to the back of the map are four portraits: *a.* Within an oval border inscribed | SICISMVNDVS I. G. TRANSYLVANIAE-MOLDA-WALACH-TRANSALPINAE-ET. SAC. ROM. IMP. PRINCEPS. SICVLORVM. COMES-PARTIVM-REGNI-HVNGARIAE-DOMINVS-AET. SVAE. XXVI. A° VERO XCVI | is a portrait of the Prince; 188 × 140 mm. (cut oval); unsigned. *b.* Within an oval border inscribed | MAXIMILIANVS D: G: ELECT: REX POL. ARCHIDVX AVST: DVX BVRG: COM. TIROL. *etc.* ORDIN: TEVT: MAGNVS MAGISTER | is a portrait of the King; 153 × 115 mm. (cut oval); n.d.; unsigned. *c.* Within an oval border inscribed | SERENISSIMVS GVILHELMVS COMES PALATINVS RHENI SVPERIORIS AC INFERIORIS BAVARIAE DVX | is a portrait of the Duke; within the oval border and beneath the portrait is the motto | IN DEO FACIEM | VIRTVTEM |; 152 × 120 mm. (cut oval); n.d.; unsigned. *d.* Within an oval border inscribed | RVDOLPHVS II. D. G. ROM. IMP. SEMPER AVG. GERMAN. HVNG. BOHEM. DALM. ETC. REX, ARCHIDVX AVSTR. DVX BVRGVND. | is a portrait of the Emperor; below the portrait | DA VICTORIAM POPVLO TVO DEVS | *Natus xv. kal. Aug. Anno* CIↃ. IↃ. LII. | *H. van Luyck excud.* |; 171 × 114 mm. (cut rectangular). On f. 125v there are four portraits: *a.* Within an oval border inscribed | CHRISTIANVS IV D. G. ELECTVS ET INAVGVRATVS REX DANIAE. NORWEG. GOTTHORVM. WAND. DVX. SLESWIG. HOLS. &: COM. OLD. ET DELM. | is a portrait of the King; within the oval border and beneath the portrait is the motto | PIETAS FVLCIT REGNA. |; 172 × 136 mm. (cut oval); n.d.; unsigned. *b.* Within an oval border inscribed | FRIDERICVS IIII. D. G. COMES PAL. RHENI. VTR. BAVARIAE DVX, SAC. ROM. IMP. DAP[ ][ ] ELECTOR SEPTEMVIR | is a portrait of the Count; within the oval border and beneath the portrait is the motto | REGE ME DOMINE SE- | CVNDVM VERBVM TVVM. |; 146 × 109 mm. (cut oval; left border cropped); 1592; unsigned [Crispin van de Passe] [See Hollstein, XV, p. 238, no. 731.] *c.* Within an oval border inscribed | FRIDERICVS WILHELMVS. D. G. ELECTORALIS ADMINISTRATOR, DVX SAXONIAE, LANDGRAV. TVRINGIAE ET MARCHIO MISNIAE|: is a portrait of the Duke; 157 × 114 mm. (cut oval); n.d.; unsigned. *d.* An oval portrait of Sigismund Bathory, Prince of Transylvania. Within the oval border and beneath the portrait is the motto | Per Idio e per la patria. |; below is the passage | IL VERO RITERATO DEL SERENIS° SIGISMONDO BATORI | PRINCIPE D'TRANSILVANIA, VALACHIA MOLDAVIA *etc.* | *H. van Luyck. exc.* |; 101 x 71 mm. (cut rectangular); n.d. On f. 126r there are four portraits: *a.* Within an oval border inscribed

| [SI]GISMVNDVS III. D. G. POLONIAE ET SVECIAE REX, MAGNVS LITHVANI[ ][ ], PRUSSIAE &c. DVX. 1595 | is a portrait of the King; within the oval border and beneath the portrait is the motto | QVO MEA ME FOR- | TVNA VOCAT. |; 140 × 110 mm. (cut oval, torn at top, cropped at left); unsigned [Similar to van de Passe; see Hollstein, XV, p. 275, no. 826.]. *b.* Within an oval border inscribed | MATTHIAS DEI GRATIA ARCHIDVX AVSTRIAE, DVX BVRGVNDIAE, COMES TIROLIS. &c. ANNO MDXCIIII | is a portrait of the Archduke; within the oval border and beneath the portrait is the motto | AMAT VICTORIA | CVRAM |; 142 × 115 mm. (cut oval, torn at top); unsigned. *c.* Within an oval border inscribed | PHILIPPVS D. G. PRINCEPS AVRANIAE, COMES A NASSAW [ ] ET DIEST | is a portrait of the Prince; 148 × 109 mm. (cut oval, torn at bottom, cropped at left); n.d.; C. Gritter. *d.* Within an oval border inscribed | MAVRITIVS D. G. NATVS AVR. PRINC. COMES NASSAVIAE, MARCHIO VEHRAE ET VLISS. GVB. PROVIN. BEL. VN. MARIS PRAEF. *etc.* | is a portrait of the Count; 149 × 119 mm. (cut oval, torn at bottom); n.d.; monogram [Crispin van de Passe] [See Hollstein, XV, p. 264, no. 792]. On f. [127]r&v there are fourteen small portraits (48 × 21 mm.) of the Roman Emperors: 127r—HENRICVS 6, PHILIPPVS, OTHO 4, FREDERICVS 2, RVDOLPHVS, ALBERTVS; 127v—HENRICVS 7, LODOWICVS, CAROLVS 4, WENCESL*aus* (these four torn at left border), ROBERTVS, SIGISMVN*dus,* ALBERTVS [2], FREDERICVS; n.d.; unsigned.

Book IV (Netherlands). Tipped to the back of the map are two engravings: *a.* Within an oval border inscribed | ISABELLA AVSTRIA, PHILIPPI II. REGIS CATHOLICI FILIA, HISPANIARVM PRINC. INFANS. | is a portrait of the Princess; below the portrait is a caption in Latin; 216 × 155 mm. (cut rectangular); n.d.; Anton. Wierex. *b.* Within an oval border is a portrait of the Cardinal Legate;

within the oval border and beneath the portrait is the passage | NATVS CIↃ. IↃ. LVIII. ID. NOVEMB. |; below is the caption | ALBERT D. D. ARCHID. AVSTRIAE, S. R. E. CARD. LEGAT. [etc.] |; 103 × 75 mm. (cut rectangular); n.d.; H. van Luyck [Similar to van de Passe; see Hollstein, XV, p. 220, no. 675.].

Book V (Spain). Tipped to the back of the map are two portraits: *a.* Philip II (see under Italy, *a.*). *b.* Within an oval border inscribed | ILLVSTRISSIMVS PHILIPPVS D. G. PRINCEPS HISPANIARVM, SERENISSIMVS PHILIPPI CATHOLICI HISP. REGIS FILIVS ANNO DOMINI MDXCIIII | is a portrait of the Prince; within the oval border and beneath the portrait is the motto | ET PATRI, ET | PATRIAE |; 146 × 110 mm. (cut oval); monogram [Crispin van de Passe] [See Hollstein, XV, p. 270, no. 807.].

Book VI (England). Tipped to the back of the map is a portrait of Elizabeth: within an oval border inscribed | ELIZABET. D. G. ANG. FRAN. HIB. ET VERG. REGINA. NATA GRONEWICIAE, ANN. M. D. XXXIII VI EID, SEPT POSVI. DEV. ADIVTOREM MEV* | is a portrait of the Queen; 153 × 118 mm. (cut oval); n.d.; unsigned [Possibly a copy after van de Passe, ca. 1592; see Hind, I, pl. 146.].

Book VII (Scotland). Tipped to the back of the map is a portrait of | THE HIGHE AND MIGHTIE PRINCE, IAMES THE SIXT, BY THE | GRACE OF GOD KINGE OF SCOTLANDE. R[enold]. E[lstrack]. fecit. |; 162 × 116 mm. (cut rectangular); n.d. [See Hind, II, p. 180.].

(Turkey). On f. 349r, within an oval border inscribed | [SVLT]AN MAHVMET III. TVRCORVM IMPERATOR INGRESSVS ANNO SALVTIS MDXCV AETATIS XXIX [ ] | is a portrait of the Sultan; within the oval border and beneath the portrait is a passage in German; 146 × 118 mm. (cut oval, cropped at top); unsigned [Crispin van de Passe] [See Hollstein, XV, p. 265, no. 798.].

Total: 54.

(F2) Book I (Italy). On f. 7v within an oval border inscribed | ss CLEMENS VIII PAPA FLORENTINVS OPT. MAX. PONTIFEX ET PRINCEPS ANNO DNI. M.D.XCVI | is a portrait of the Pope; 111 × 85 mm. (cut oval); Crispin van de Passe; see under (F1) Engravings, Italy. On f. 33r within an oval border inscribed | PHILIPPVS II. CAR. V. FIL. HISPAN. IND. NEAP. SICIL. HIEROSOL. &c. REX CATHOL. MED. BRAB. GELD. DVX, FLAND. HOLL. HAN. COMES &c | is a portrait of the King; within the oval border and beneath the portrait is the motto | DOMINVS MIHI | ADIVTOR |; 146 × 115 mm. (cut oval); n.d.; unsigned [This portrait served as the model for the Overadt map; see under (F2) Maps, Spain.]. On f. 58r is a portrait of Paschalis Ciconia Dux Venetorum; 111 × 84 mm. (cut oval) [See under (F1) Engravings, Italy.]. On ff. 75r–79r are sixty-five portraits of the Roman Emperors: C. IVL CAESAR, OCT. AVGVST., CLAVDIVS, CAIVS CALI., TIBERIVS AV., NERO CLAV., VESPASIANVS, TITVS, DOMITANVS, NERVA, TRAIANVS, HADRIANVS, ANTONIVS P., MARVR. ANTO., COMMODVS, L. SEP. SEṼR., CARACALLA, ELIOGABALVS, ALEXANDER, MAXIMINVS, GORDIANVS, M. IVL. PHILIPPVS, TRAIANVS, VIBIVS, AEMILIANVS, VALERIVS MA., CLAVDIVS, AVRELIANVS, TACITVS, PROBVS, CARVS, DIOCLETIAN, CONSTANTIVS, MAXENTIVS, CONSTANTÑS, CONSTANTINVS, CONSTANTIVS, CONSTANS, IVLIANVS, IOVINIANVS, VALENTINIA, GRATIANVS, THEODOSIVS, ARCADIVS, HONORIVS, THEODOSIVS 2, VALENTINIA, MARTINIANVS, LEO, ZENO, MAVRITIVS, FOCAS, HERACLIVS, CONSTANS 2, CONSTANTI IV, IVSTINANVS 2, PHILIPPICVS, ANASTASI 2, LEO, LEO CONS:; 46 × 28 mm.; n.d.; unsigned.

Book III (Germany). On ff. 176r–179r are thirty-nine portraits of the Roman Emperors: CAROLVS MAG.,

HVLDOWICVS, LOTARIVS, LODOWICVS, CARO: CAL:, CAROL: CRAS:, ARNOLPHVS, LVDOWICVS, HENRICVS 1, OTHO *Magnus,* OTHO 2, OTHO 3, HEINRICVS 2, CONRADVS, HEINRICVS 2[3], HEINRICVS 3[4], HENRICVS 5, LOTTARIVS, CONRADVS, BARBAROSSA, HEINRICVS 6, PHILIPPVS, OTHO 5, FREDERICVS 2, RVDOLPHVS, ALBERTVS, HENRICVS 7, LODOWICVS, CAROLVS 4, WENCESL*aus,* ROBERTVS, SIGISMVN*dus,* ALBERTVS 2, FREDERICVS, MAXIMIL*ianus,* CAROLVS, FERDINAN*dus,* MAXIMIL*ianus,* RVDOPHVS; 46 × 28 mm.; n.d.; unsigned.

Books VI, VII, VIII: Tipped to the rear sides of the maps of England, Scotland, and Ireland is a three-quarter-length portrait of James I, in body armor and hat, standing in the center with a table on the left on which is a plumed helmet; on the right stands another table with the four crowns of the empire atop; above is the arms of the empire; the above margin contains a pedigree of James's descent from Henry VII; inscribed in the lower margin | *The most High, and Mighty Prince* IAMES *by the grace* | *of god King of England Scotland France, and Ireland,* | *Defender of the faith &c. Natus 1566. Iuny 19.* | *H. Woutnel Excud. Beniamin W*[right]. *fecit after his trw pickter.* |; 222 × 160 mm. (cut rectangular); n.d. [1603]; Benjamin Wright. [See W. R. Streitberger, "A New Benjamin Wright Engraving," *The Library,* 28 (1973), 327–28.]

Total: 110.

VII. COATS OF ARMS

F1 contains 2,556 emblazoned coats of arms, 572 of which are 19th century additions; F2 contains 2,126 coats, four of which are later additions (see Handwriting, other hands, below, for a detailed description of the additions).[2] The majority of the hand-painted coats, those on leaves with printed rules in the catalogues of nobility, measure 40 × 33 mm.; those in the margins of the text, including those in the F2 chronology of Germany, measure between 40 to 50 × 33 to 36 mm.; those in the remaining chronologies measure between 13 to 15 × 16 to 19 mm. The arms are distributed as follows:

Book I (Italy): F1—11 on t.p., 19 in margins, 233 in catalogue; F2—11 on t.p., 19 in margins, 122 in catalogue.

Book II (France): F1—16 on t.p., 72 in margins, 168 in catalogue; F2—15 on t.p., 81 in margins, 129 in catalogue.

Book III (Germany): F1—17 on t.p., 75 in margins, 367 in catalogue; F2—17 on t.p., 80 in margins, 134 in catalogue.

Book IV (Netherlands): F1—19 on t.p., 22 in margins, 24 in catalogue; F2—19 on t.p., 18 in margins, 141 in catalogue.

Book V (Spain): F1—13 on t.p., 43 in margins, 187 in catalogue; F2—13 on t.p., 76 in margins, 119 in catalogue.

Book VI (England): F1—10 on t.p., 198 in margins, 832 in catalogue; F2—10 on t.p., 198 in margins, 566 in catalogue.

Book VII (Scotland): F1—1 on t.p., 19 in margins, 223 in catalogue; F2—1 on t.p., 39 in margins, 257 in catalogue.

Book VIII (Ireland): F1—1 on t.p., 23 in margins, 82 in catalogue; F2—1 on t.p., 21 in margins, 80 in catalogue.

VIII. HANDWRITING

Scribes: Four scribes were employed to prepare F1 and six to prepare F2. While the chronologies of each book of the manuscript are written mainly in italic, the bulk of the manuscript is written in secretary script with italic forms scattered throughout to distinguish proper names, foreign phrases and section headings. Tables of contents, running titles, and some division headings are rendered in ornamental gothic script.

(F1) Scribe A wrote a large cursive secretary and italic, employing black ink that has faded to brown in a few places. He is responsible for the text and chronology of Italy—4r–68r; the text of France—44r–74v; and probably for the chronology of Spain—184r–193v. Scribe B wrote a medium, more angular secretary, employing a brown ink which shows watery when thin. He is responsible for the text of Germany—95r–125r; the text of the Netherlands—145r–159r; the text of Spain—169r–183v; and probably for [iv]r. Scribe C wrote a small cursive secretary which is slightly more angular than A's, employing brown ink. He wrote the text of England and Wales—204r–252v; the text of Scotland—300r–312r; the text of Ireland—339r–344v; the chronology of England—253r–256r; the chronology of Scotland—312r–316r; the fragment on Turkey—349r&v; and probably the text of Burgundy—159v; the tables for Spain—199r–200r; and the tables for England—333r–334v. Scribe D wrote a cursive secretary, employing ink which varies from brown to dark brown. He is responsible for the preliminary material—[ii]r–[iii]v; the chronology for France—76r–78v; and for the chronology of Germany—127r&v.

(F2) Scribe A wrote a large, graceful secretary with a full six-mm space between the lines, writing about forty lines of twelve words to a page, employing a dark brown ink. He is responsible for the text and index of Italy—1r–72v; the text and index of the Netherlands—199v–265v; the text, chronology, and index of Spain—214r–240v; and the chronology and index of England—

316r&v, 321r–322v. Scribe B wrote a large broad secretary heavily shaded on the downstrokes. He employed abbreviations more frequently than A, and gets thirty-eight lines of twelve words to a page. He is responsible for the text and chronology of France—89r–122v, 125r–134v; the chronology of Germany—176r–179r; the notes on the nobility of Scotland—378r–383r; and possibly the note on export-import for Italy—70v. Scribe C wrote with a brownish-black ink which shows brown when thin; he gets forty-seven lines of thirteen words to a page; he is unique among the scribes for the virtual lack of abbreviations. He is responsible for the text of Germany—139r–173v. Scribe D when pressed for space wrote a very small angular secretary with numerous abbreviations, although he usually wrote forty-three lines of thirteen words to a page. He had a tendency to employ synaloepha; he began with a thin, light brown ink which he exchanged for black on 285r. He wrote the text of England—249r–296v, 315r&v; and probably the chronology of England—317r–320v. Scribe E wrote a broad, graceful secretary with black ink which shows grey when thin. The broad strokes and, despite the full five-mm space between lines, the descenders which penetrate the lines below make the hand somewhat difficult to read. His work is distinguished also by the still visible pencil guidelines suggesting that he may not have been a professional scribe. He wrote the remaining portion of the text of England—297v–314v; and the text for Scotland—346r–351v. Scribe F's letter forms are similar to A's, but the overall characteristics of the hand are sufficiently different to distinguish the two. He wrote a small graceful secretary in black ink, although some patches of his work appear in brown. Usually he wrote sixty-four lines of sixteen words to a page but, on occasion, only forty-five lines. He wrote the text of the Netherlands—199r–205v; the text of Scotland—352r–365v; the text of Ireland—390r–396r; and possibly the chronology of Italy—75r–79v; a note in the text of England—321r; and some of the preliminary material—[iii]r–[iv]r.

Other hands: (F1) 572 nineteenth-century additions are made to the catalogues of nobility of England and Scotland; the additions range from one-word supplements to Tyllney's notes to entire coats of arms and notes (see Coats of Arms). The handwriting varies considerably, yet they were in all probability made by Thomas Willement (see History of the Manuscripts); most of the additions record creations after September 1776 and the last death notice on 4 February 1782. The additions occur on ff. 258r&v, 259v, 260r–261v, 263r–266v, 268r–270r, 271v, 273r–274r, 275v–276r, 277r–279r, 280r&v, 282v, 284r, 285r–286r, 287v, 290v–291v, 293r&v, 295r&v, 296v–297r, and 318r.

(F2) 1. On the third binder's leaf the title of the manuscript is written in a late eighteenth- or early nineteenth-century cursive hand. 2. An eighteenth- or nineteenth-century hand, in grey ink, watery colors, and amateur emblazoning talents, is responsible for the following additions: f. 325r | [Breuse] of xxxx Clack-manen an antient famelie in the King-dome of Scotland./ [coat of arms is 17th century] |; f. 378v | Glasse of Galke in the Shiresdome of Aberdeene; an antient famelie in Scotland/ [coat of arms] |; f 380v. | Marshall of that Ilke an antient famelie in Scotland/ [coat of arms] |; 381r | Pont of Shiresmill in the Shirresdome of Clackmanan in Scotland; descended of a Franch race/ |. 3. A seventeenth or early eighteenth-century italic hand, using brown ink is responsible for: f. 327v | [Euers] This is an ancient family. |; f. 334v | Palmer of Angmerin in Sussex an Antient famely: Wingham in Kent is now the Cheife House: |. 4. An eighteenth-century cursive hand, in a faded brown ink, is responsible for: f. 334v | [Palmer] from hence is descended ye Earle of Castlemayne, 1661: |.

Tyllney: Tyllney has added material both in the text and margins of F1; his pencil directions are still visible under the scribes' ink in the notes to the nobility. For F2 he provided additions in both pencil and ink; he provided the indexes for France, Germany, and Scotland. He acted as proofreader and corrector for both manuscripts. The following is a list of his substantive additions (E, erasure; +, added to the same line; wo, write over; △, added above line; ▽, added below line; C, cancel; P, pencil, >, direction of revision; x, for each undeciphered letter):

(F1) ff. [ii]r Q:Foll: x21 (+), Q:Foll: 80/ (+), Q Foll: 86. (+), now (△); [ii]v Q Foll: 50/ 176/ 188/ (+), Q. Foll: (I) 50/127/156/188/278 (P,+); [iii]v off (△), off ye land (△); 4r silkes (△); 7r who (+); 10r pbem > plebm (△); 10v The Sea off Rome (+), Aldobrabdini (+); 11r other (△); 20r afterwardes (△); 22r hill (△); 22v w^{t} > wher In is (wo,△); 24v but > yet (wo), viz (△); 25r de Medices (+); 27v Vrbine (+); 30r Ferrare (+); 31v [Ge]nua (+); 32r longe (+), miñgled (C,△); 33r Spayne (+), Sic̀ellie (+); 33v xx > / /who (E,wo); 34r his (△); 35r base (△); 42v townes (△); 43r Lombardie (+); 45r vntill xxxxxx (C), xx > being (wo); 46v [Mo]ntferratto (+); 47r The Marquezes of Saluz (+), Salus (+), Mirandula (+); 47v Parma (+); 49r Inhabitants wheroff (△); 49v [M]antua (+); 50r Sicelie (+); 51v Venice (+), Grimanni (+); 54v think (△); 59v for y^{em}selues (△); 60v–61v [numbers to the index] (+); 64v he (△); 70r plebeyans (+); 70v–38r [traces of pencil notes written over by scribes in ink] (+); 72r Gibelines (+), Cazza (+); 72v Crapera (+,P); 74r & who haue sought much to tiraniz (+), Guelphes (+), Plebeians (+); 74v Guelphes (+); 78r Gibeline (+), Guelphes (+); 44r had (△), but (△), * or 200 frenche Leages by othr (+); 45r By w^{h} ciuell warres (△), hertofor (+), Arlles (+); 46r not only (△); 46v Kinge (△), still (△); 50r ment (△); 51r marrishe (△); 51v Bolloygne (+), Vermendois

(+), Vnto (△), Erldom (△), Agayn (+), King (△), he (△), vnto/ (+); 52r St. Polle (+); 53r Normandie (+), Vallois (+); 53v Longoville (+); Eu (+), Euereux (+), Harcourt (+), Aumall (+); 54r wherby (wo); 54v Nemoux (+), [M]omerancie (+), Descended (△); 55r Mounfort (+); 56r Champayne (+), more (△); 56v Barr (+), Angwien (+), Guyss (+), Vadamont (+), Wheroff (△); 57r Lignie (+), Bryen (+), Auxerra (+); 57v Rethell (+); 58r Brittayn (+); 58v Porhoett (+); 60v Orleans (+), Berrie (+), Estampes (+), Anioe (+); 61r Chartres (+), Vandosme (+); 61v Bloys (+); 62v Burgandie-Pall (+); 63r × > yt famely (wo,△), Burgudie D: (+); 63v Charralois (+), Charnye (+); 65v Aquitayn (+); 66r Aquitane (+), Angulesme (+), Arminiach (+), Arminiach/ (+); 66v Perdriach (+), Albrett (+), Candalle (+); 68r Borbon (+), Mompensier (+), Neuers (+); 68v Auergina (+); 69v Tholowze (+), Foyxe (+); 70v Vienois (+), Oraynge (+); 71r Valentinois (+); 71v Provance (+); 72v Lorayn Antiq (+), [L]orayn modern (+); 74r Savoye (+); 77r Ethelwlph (+); 78r off 26 gentilmen w^{t} out dep[ ] (△); 80r–90v [pencil notes written over by scribes in ink] (+); 82r &[Candum]ois off ye houss off Foix (P,+); 89v w^{t} In ye government off orlleans (P,+); 95v parted Into diuerse branches first/ viz: Ysel: wael & *Leak,* etc. (+), noted to bee/ (+); 100v [wh]om they except In all [C]onfedracies w^{t} other princes/ (+); 103r ye cutrie (wo,△), & coper (△); 105v [pencil traces under note] (+); 106v to be (+), but vnder ye Ecclesi[astic]all Iurisdiction off Bamberg [and F]ranconia/ (+); 110v noted to be ye Capitall towne in Wederaw/ (+); 112v Accoũted to be ye greatest cetty In Germany (+), In misina (△), w^{t} In ye Iurisdiction wheroff are diuers mynes off Siluer/(+), A capitall seatt off ye Princes off Hassia (+); 114v besides ye DD: of Saxony (+), ther be ye Earlles off Ravenspurge, Marche, Benthem, Terklelburg, Sleyword, Lippiam, Spigetburge, & Piermontayn/ wch last 3 are latly vnited by marriage Into one, wherunto are adioyned as members of Westfalia ye Earlles off Reythberg, Oldenbur, & Delmenhurst (+); 115r [pencil traces under scribes' ink] (+); 124v as It is noted/ (+); 130r–141v [pencil traces under scribes' ink] (+); 134r Graue In (P), Heren (P); 138v descended fro (P), descended frõ (P); 140v [two pencil additions too light to decipher] (+); 141v In Sevia (P); 159r&v Ayxe (+), Cambraye (+), Lege (+), Mabewge (+), [ ][I]s now vnited vnto ye cause off Spayn w^t^ ye other vnited provinces (P,+); 160r–161v [pencil traces under scribes' ink]; 161r de Tylling (P,+); 170r by sum oppinions (△); 171r vntill now off late (△), rated att 2 millions more (△), besides (△); 174r, 175v, 179v [pencil traces under scribes' ink]; 183r Callatuit (+), Compostella (+), Carthago 177 (+); 183v Segouia (+), St Ovales (+), Oscha (+), Tarrascona (+), Vcles (+); 186r Sũ dow [set] dow̃ his [ ] alphons [ ] haue ra[ ] before In [ ] (+); 194r–198v [pencil traces under scribes' ink] (+); 195r seated In Castella & Teracona (P,+); 204v bothe (wo), off them (△); 209r "arbiter (+); 210v sayd (△), still (+); 216v Lushere (+), Ligh (+), Gauell (+); 222v Graie (+), In Staffordsh * (+); 225v [ink over Tyllney's pencil] rayne of k E ye 6. Q mary and Q. Elizabeth (+); 226r but Athelstayne subdued ye whole Cũtrie In Ano 926/ / / (+); 238r&v lyttlebury/ (+), Paynell/ (+), Tonney (+), Muson/ (+), Lamto (+); 239v Peuerell (△); 249r / / In whose posteritie It Continueth (P,+); 250r & now (△); 251r of ye Layetie (+); 254r he maried ye daughter off Charles 2: K off Fr— (+); 255r hauing (△); 256r Burford (+), Elmsley (+); 256v E. Grymsted (+), Hampton Court (+), Keswik (+), Leynster (+), Manchester (+), Norham (+), Oxford (+), Southwark (+), Tenbye (+), The Vieze (+), Woodstock (+), Warwick (+); 257r–297v [pencil traces under scribes' ink] (+); 262r In Lecestersher (+); 275v In reasonable good state (P,+); 290r And ye L Spencer made Knight of ye Garter temp Ed 3 (P,+); 300v North Scotland (+), West Scotland (+); 312r & strangled by his nobles (+), w^{t}out Succession (+); 312v for tiranny (+), & died w^{t}out successiõ (+), by sum opinions he was Crathlints brothers son (+), being ye 39 king off ye Scottes frõ ye first Fergus; 313v slayn by ye Pights (+), & first recorded ye Acts of Scotlad (+), & slew herselff—(+), buried in Icolmekell (+), & died off ye gowtt buried at Icolmekell (+), buried at Icolmekell/ (+), Buried In Icolmekill (+), slayn Secretly by ye shott off an arrow (+); 314r wher he died (+), & pacified all ye vpprors In his own Lande (+); 314v he was ye first prince buried In Duferling/ (+), he (△), & buried In Duñfermeling Abby (+), & descesid w^{t}out Succession (+), & renued ye Leage w^{t} frañc (+), & was buried att Dũfermeling (+), homag (+), w^{t}outt succession (+), sõ dow sett dow̃ 3 Alexãders (+); 315r In France (+); 315v buried In St Iohns tow̃ (+); 345r–348v [pencil traces under scribes' ink]; 349r 13 yeres w^{t} his own hand in Anõ Dñi 1403 ye 3^{d} yere off his Imprisonment/ (+)

(F2) ff. 3v therby (△); 4r being (△), afterward (△); 7v The Sea off Rome (+), Aldobrandini (+); 22r Florens (+); 23r de Medices (+); 26r Vrbyne (+); 29r Ferrara Antiche (+), Ferrara Moderne (+); 31v Genua (+); 33r Spayne (+), Neaples (+); 45r miles (△); 46v Spayne, & Lũbard (+); 50r Palleolgus (+); 51v Farnesse (+); 53v Inhabitants wheroff (△); 54r Gonzaga (+); 58r Venice (+), Grimani (+); 68r Impregnable (+); 76r he (△); 76v y^{e} (△), ded (△); 79r negligent (+); 79v wheroff (△); 81r a greate famelie (P,+); 82r Fregosi (P,+), The Fabiani (P,+); 83r [pencil addition too light to decipher] (+), Negra (P,+); 83v Orio (P,+), [pencil addition too light to decipher] (+); 84r Sant Vitale (P,+); 118r Sea (△); 123r&v [Complete index for France] (+); 125r Franconia (+), Frañs Antiq (+); 125v Frañs moder̃ (+); 126v Pepen (+); 127r Charlemaỹ (+); 127v France (+); 128r Castell (+); 128v Navare (+), Burgãdy: C (+), Vallois (+); 129r Burgãdy D: (+); 129v France (+), Englande (+), Orleans (+); 130r Brittayn (+), Scotlãd (+); 130v Borbone (+);

142v the ꝑ (+); 148v the (+); 149v ye vpper (+); 154r for (△); 174r&v [complete index for Germany] (+); 187r [pencil directions for emblazoning coats of arms]; 189r lyue (△); 191r hauen (△); 197v Inherytance/ (+); 203r Issued (△); 205v Zutphen (+), Zerburge (+); 206r–209v [pencil traces under scribes' ink] (+); 226v vallued att 70^{m} duc p Anũ (+), vallued att 48^{m} duc p Anũ (+); 228v vppẽ (+); 231v Segouia (+); 232r Leon (+) 232r Nauar (+), Gallicia (+), & desceasid (△); 233r Castella (+); 233v Tholouz (+), Leone (+); 234v Arragõ (+), Austria (+); 235r Navarr (+), Arragon (+); 235v Castella (+), Arragon (+), Navarr (+), Navarr (+); 236r Chãpayn (+), Fraunce (+), Eureuxe (+), Arragon (+); 236v Foyxe (+), Albrette (+), Borbon (+), Arragon (+), Arragon (+); 236r Barcelona (+), Valentia (+), Sicely (+); 236v Castella (+); 237r Neaples (+), Portugall (+); 237v Algraue (+), Portugal (+); 241v–243r [pencil traces under scribes' ink] (+); 256v The ꝑtecular (+); 257r Vortiger (P,+); 260r Wilnotus (+), Odo (+), Flanders (+), kentte (+), Plantaginet (+); 260v Hollande (+), Graye (+); 262r Montgomery (+), as diuers other noble howses maye likwise pretend/ (P,+); 262v Dabignie (+), Fitzallen (+), Ratcliffe (+), In right off ye Elder sister (P,+); 264r Warrene (+), de Egle (+), Plantaginet/ (+); 265r Glanville (+); 265v Vfforde (+), de la Pole (+), Brandon (+); 266r Clare (+), Plantaginet (+), Plantaginett (+); 267r Bigott (+), Plantaginett (+), Mowbraye (+); 267v Howardd (+); 268v Plantaginet (+); 269v Cadore (+); Cornwale (+), Plantaginet (+); 271r Brewere (+), Riuers (+), Courtney (+), Hollande (+); 271v Courtnay (+); 272r (Graye (+); 273r *Mohun* (+), *Bewfortt* (+); 273v Seymoure (+), Daubney (+), Bowrchere (+); 274v Scrowpe (+), Stafford (+), Stafford (+), Butler (+), Bulleyn (+); 275r Bloys (+), Longspee (+), Lacy (+), Montacutt (+), Nevell (+); 276r Siward (+), Gobbion (+), Fitzwilliams (+), Wriotesley (+), Quinsaye (+), Spencer (+), Paullett (+), graced (△), aboue 20

(+); 277r Hungerforde (+); 279v Estoutvile (+), Guelffus (+), Plantaginet (+), Guelffe (△); 280r Champaine (+), Brittayne (+); 281v Plantaginett (+); 282r Plantaginett (+); 282v Nevell (+), de Foixe (+); 283v Mischeynes (+), Clifforde (+); 284v Waldeoffe (+), Mowbray (+), Scotland (+), Percie (+); 287r Maundevile (+); 287v Ludgarshall (+), Fitzpers (+), Bowcher (+), Deuereaux (+); 290r de Glocester (+), de Clare/ (+), Montherm^{r} (+), Gavestõ (+), Audleye (+); 290v Plantaginett (+), Spencere (+); 291v Edgar Ethelinge (+), Vere (+); 292v Gifforde (+), Stafforde (+); 293r de Coussie (+), Plantaginet (+), Nevill (+), Tewdore (+), Russell (+); 294r Parre (+), Wooduile (+); 294v Manares (+,E,wo); 297r Marcare (+), Romare (+), Quinsay (+), Lacye (+), de-la-poole (+), Brandon (+), Fines (+); 297v de Gaut (+), Fitzwith (+), Vmfrevile (+); 298r Peuerelle (+), Howarde (+); 299r Stanley (+), Kennelworth (+); 299v Tarquinus (+), de Beamot (+), de Placetis (+), Maduitt (+), Beauchamp (+), *Vrsois* (+); 300r Neville (+), Sutton (+), Dudleye (+); 301r de Abcot (+), Percie (+), Bewchap (+), Tiptofte (+), Somersette (+); 301v Stafforde (+); 302v de Montgomerie (+), Talbotte (+); 303v Lupus (+), Bohume (+), Scotteland (+); 304r Waldeoff (+), Sent-lis (+), Scotland (+); 304v Clynton (+), Hastinges (+); 305r The principallitie off Walles (+); 307v De Lacie (+), Mortimere (+), Dudley (+); 308v Griffethe (+), Southwalles (+); 310r de Ogie (+), Marshall (+), Valence (+), Hastinges (+); 310v Harbartt (+); 311r Harbartt (+); 311v Bohum (+), Brewss (+), Stafford (+); 312r Mortimere (+); 313r Osborne (+), Fitzwalter (+); 313v Bohume (+); 316r Caseuilan (+), Rome (+), Rome (+), Crassus (+), octauiꝰ (+), Gratiaṅꝰ (+); 316v Constatin (+), Vortiger (+), k: Arther (+), Malgo (+), Cadwan (+), *Soueragtie* (+), his (△); 317r Inas (+), Kynulphꝰ (+), Egbartt (+), west saxony (+), Athelstaỹ (+); 317v Ironside (+), Knutt (+); 318r westsaxony (+), Harrold (+), Normandie (+); 318v Bloyse (+), Plantaginet (+), Normadie

& Aquitayn (+); 319v France & Englande (+), Lacaster (+); 320r Yorke (+); 322r Sandwiche (+); 316r–321r [date and regnal year columns] (+); 321r–322v [numbers to index] (+); 323v–339r [pencil traces under scribes' ink and pencil directions for emblazoning coats of arms] (+); 324v frõ whõ Is Descẽded Bradborn off Bradborn In Derbysher (P,+); 331r Kaivile (P,+); 331v Latham (P,+); 332v from whõ Is descẽded Mõgomery off Sussex (P,+); 337r Brues (P,+); 351v town (△); 352v Quinsay (+), Balleoll (+), Dowglas (+); 353r Dowglass (+), Brewsse (+), Dunbarr (+); 353v Stywarde (+), Dowglas (+), Montgomerie (+), Kenedie (+); 354v Campbelle (+), Lenox (+); 355r Styarde (+), Hamilton (+), Cuninghame (+); 356r Stywarde (+), Gordone (+), Sowtherland (+); 356v Sinclare (+), Orknaye (+); 358v Stywarde (+), Dowglas (+); 359r Stywarde (+), Haye (+), Stywarde (+), Lindsaye (+); 359v Keythe (+), Lisleye (+), Arreskyne (+), Greame (+); 360r Rethwyne (+), Greame (+); 361r–369v [date and regnal year columns] (+); 362v Scotland (+); 363v England (+), Waldeoff (+); 364r Balleoll (+); 364v Brewss (+), Styward (+); 366r [complete index for Scotland] (+).

IX. CONDITION

The spine of F1 is broken; its covers are detached; the edges of its pages are bent; its maps torn; and parts of the text are missing.

The leather at the spine on the front cover of F2 is beginning to break and the front binder's leaves have loosened. The ink has penetrated the leaves in places but not so much as to preclude deciphering the text. Aside from these defects the manuscript is in remarkably good condition.

VIII
Descriptive Index

F1, the earlier of the two authorially supervised and corrected manuscripts, has accidental authority (i.e., in matters of spelling, punctuation, capitalization, etc.). This manuscript, prepared by scribes between 1597 and 1601 from Tyllney's drafts, preserves more of his accidentals than F2, which was prepared by other scribes working from F1 and revised drafts as their copy. The scribes have followed their own practices which accounts for the sometimes wide variation in accidentals even within each of the individual books of the work. There are roughly one in six accidental variations between F1 and F2, but Tyllney personally supervised and corrected both manuscripts and approved of the texts.

F1 is not complete. Parts of the text are missing and other parts are made up of notes and documents used as the basis for the revisions in F2. Tyllney's final substantive intentions, in so far as they are realized, are witnessed by F2.

The following index is designed to coordinate information found in both versions of the work. In cases where Tyllney's chapter title does not clearly indicate the subject treated, I provide a brief explanation. The following abbreviations and symbols are used: top. desc.—topographical description; succ.—succession of peers; hist.

desc.—historical description; pol. desc.—political description; econ. hist.—economic history; frag.—fragment; [ ]—editorial interpolation.

F1		F2
	[Preliminary Material]	
[i^v–iii^v]	Four tables [see above, p. 21]	om.
[iv^r]	Villicationis Ratio (F1) Perigrinationis Ratio (F2)	[ii^r]
[iv^v]	[Table of Contents]	[ii^v]
om.	[Dedication]	[iii^r]
2r	Book I. Ittalie	[iv^r]
2v	[Table of Contents]	[iv^v]
4r–v	The generale Discription of Ittalie	1r–2r
5r–6r	The pryncypall Navygable and boundynge Ryuers of Ittalye	2r–3r
6r–8r	The gouermente of Ittalie in general [Hist. from Romulus to the early 17th cent.]	3r–5r
8r	The Romaine Lawes	5r
8r–10r	The Common Wealthe and Pollicie of the Romannes [Hist. desc. of the offices, political divisions, and social classes of Rome]	5r–7r
10r	The particulare Discription of Ittalie, accordinge Vnto the seuerall Prouinces therof, now deuided into nineteine Regions	7r
10r	[Table of ancient and modern names for the 19 provinces]	7r
10v–11v	The Sea of Rome otherwise called Sainct Peters Patrimony for ther Temporallities in Ittalie, as yt was in the greatest pryde of that Sea [Hist. account of the political rise of the Papacy, an assessment of its methods of governing, its income, and fortifications]	7v–8v

F1		F2
11v–20v	The Papacie of Rome and Churche Regimente in Ittalie [Annotated chronology of the Popes focusing on their political struggles in the accumulation of temporal power]	8v–18v
20v–22v	Campania de Roma [top. desc.]	18v–20r
22v–24r	Tuscan or Hetruria [top. desc.]	20v–23v
24r–25v	The gouermente of fflorence	22r–23v
25v–26r	Vmbria [top. desc.]	24r–v
26v–27v	The Marquezate of Anconitana [top. desc.]	24v–26r
27v	The Dukes of Vrbin [succ.]	26r
28r–30r	Romania [top. desc.]	26v–29r
30r–v	The Dukes of fferrar [succ.]	29r–30r
30v–31v	Liguria Transalpenina [top. desc.]	30r–31r
31v–32v	The gouerment of Genua [pol. and econ. hist.]	31r–32v
32v	The Marquesses of ffinario [succ.]	32v
33r–v	The Spanishe Regiment in Ittalie [Spanish revenue and expenses associated with maintaining garrisons and defenses in Italy]	33r–v
33v–36r	The kingdome of Neaples [pol. hist.]	33v–37r
36r–37r	Campania Antica [top. desc.]	37r–38v
37r–v	Lucania [top. desc.]	38v–39r
37v–38v	The Loar Calabria [top. desc.]	39r–40v
38v–39v	The Higher Calabria [top. desc.]	40v–42r
40r–v	The Lande of Otranto [top. desc.]	42v–43v
40v–41v	The Lande of Barr [top. desc.]	43v–44v
41v–42v	Puglia the Champion [top. desc.]	44v–45v
42v–43r	Abruzzo [top. desc.]	45v–46v
43r–44v	Lumbardy [succ.]	46v–48v
44v–46v	Lumbardy Cispadana [top. desc.]	49r–50r
46v–47r	The Marques of Montferratto [succ.]	50r–51r
47r	The Marquezes off Saluz [succ.]	om.
47r–v	The Earles of Mirandula [succ.]	51r
47v	The Dukes of Parma [succ.]	51v
48r–49v	Lumbardie Transpadana [top. desc.]	52r–54r
49v	The Dukes of Mantua [succ.]	54r–v
49v–50r	The principallitie off Pie-montt [top. desc. and succ.]	54v–56r

F1		F2
50r–51r	Sicilie a Member of Ittalie and Vnder the Spanishe Regiment [top. desc. and military desc.]	56r–57r
51r	Sardegna [top. desc.]	57r–v
51v–52v	The Signorie of Venice [pol. hist. and diplomatic relations]	58r–59v
52v–54v	The Gouerment of Venice	59v–62v
54v–56r	The pollicie of Venice for the Administration of Iustice both in Ciuill and Criminall Causes	62v–64v
56r	The Populare State of Venice [offices held by commoners and class relations]	64v–65r
56r–v	The Venetian gouermente Within Terra Ferma [government structure in Venetian cities and territories abroad]	65r
56v–58r	Marca Triugiana [top. desc.]	65r–67v
58v–59r	The Duchie of ffriuli [top. desc.]	68r–v
59r–v	The Gouerment of ffriuly [succ.]	68v–69r
59v	The Marquizat of Istria [top. desc.]	69r–v
59v–60r	The Principall famulies aswell of the Venetians as allso vnder the venetian gouermente	69v–70r
om.	What Ware and Marchandize are Ordinarielie Carried out off Ittalie Into oure parts and What they Retourne againe	70r
60v–61v	[Index]	71r–72v
62r–68r	[Annotated chronology of the Roman Emperors and Kings from Romulus to 781 A.D.]	73r–79v
70r–79r, 38r–v	[Coats of arms and notes on the chief families of Italy]	81r–84v
43r	Book II. ffrance withe the Confronting Provancs Allied therto	88r
43v	[Table of Contents]	88v
44r–45r	The generall Discription of ffrance	89r–90r

F1		F2
45r	The Principall Nauigable and bounding Riuers of France	90v
45v–46v	The Regimente of France in generall	91r–92r
46v–48r	The lawes of ffrance with the Publike Administration therof	92v–94r
48r–49r	The Reueneues, and Profitts of the Crowne of ffrance, dewe vnto the kinge, with the manner of the leueinge therof and the Courts apperteyning thervnto	94r–95r
49r–50r	The Pollicie of France, for the publike gouermente of that state, and dewe Administration of Iustice within the same	95r–96v
50r–v	The Principall officers and severall gardes with other Court Attendants for the kings Person and Housholde	96v
50v	The Particuler Description of France According Vnto the severall Provances therof devided into 12 gouermentes	96v
50v	[Index to the 12 governments]	97r
50v–51v	The Gouermente of Piccardy [top. desc.]	97r–98r
51v	The Earldome of Bolloygn [succ.]	98r
51v	The Earles of Vermendois [succ.]	98r
52r	The Earles of St. Poll [succ.]	98v
52r–53r	The Gouermente of Normandie [top. desc.]	98v–99v
53r	Normandie [succ.]	100r
53r–v	Alonson and Vallois [succ.]	100r
53v	Longouille [succ.]	100r
53v	Eu [succ.]	100v
53v	Eureux [succ.]	100v
53v	Harcourte [succ.]	100v
53v	Aumale [succ.]	100v
54r–v	The Ile of ffrance [top. desc.]	101r–v
54v	Nemoux [succ.]	101v
54v	Momorancie and Domartin [succ.]	102r
55r	Mounforte [succ.]	102r

F1		F2
55r–56r	The gouermente of Champayn and Brye [top. desc.]	102r–103r
56r–v	The Earles of Champayn [succ.]	103r–v
56v	The Earles of Barr [succ.]	103v
56v	The Earles of Anguien [succ.]	103v–104r
56v	The Earles of Guise [succ.]	104r
56v	The Earles of Vadamont [succ.]	104r
57r	The Earles of Lignie [succ.]	104r–v
57r	The Earles of Bryen [succ.]	104v
57r	The Earles of Auxerre [succ.]	104v
57v	The Earles of Rethell [succ.]	104v
57v–58r	The Gouermente of Brittaine [top. desc.]	105r–v
58r–v	The Dukes of Brittaine [succ.]	105v–106r
58v	The Earles of Porhoet [succ.]	106r
58v–60v	The gouerment of Orleance [top. desc.]	106r–108r
60v	The Dukes of Orleans [succ.]	108r–v
60v	The Dukes of Berry [succ.]	108v
60v	The Dukes of Estampes [succ.]	108v
60v–61r	The Dukes of Anjoe and Tourayne [succ.]	108v–109r
61r	The Earles of Chartres [succ.]	109r
61r–v	The Earles of Vandosme [succ.]	109r–v
61v	The Earles of Bloys [succ.]	109v
61v–62v	The Gouerment of Burgundie [top. desc.]	109v–110v
62v–63r	The Counte Pallatin of Burgundie [succ.]	110v–111r
63r–v	The Dukedome of Burgundie [succ.]	111r–v
63v	The Earles of Charralois [succ.]	111v
63v	The Earles of Charnie [succ.]	111v
63v–65v	The Gouermente of Guyen [top. desc.]	111v–114r
66r	The Dukes of Aquitaine [succ.]	114r
66r	The Earles of Angulesme [succ.]	114r
66r–v	The Earles of Arminiach [succ.]	114v
66v	The Countie of Perdriach [succ.]	114v
66v	The Countie of Albrett [succ.]	114v
66v	The Earles of Kendall or Candall [succ.]	114v

F1		F2
66v–67r	The Gouerment of Lionois and Auergina [top. desc.]	115r–v
68r	The Earles of Borbon and Clermonte [succ.]	115v–116r
68r	The Counties of Monpansere [succ.]	116r
68r–v	The Dukes of Neuers [succ.]	116r
68v	The Countie Dolphine of Auergina and Forrestes [succ.]	116r–v
68v–69r	The Gouermente of Languidoc [top. desc.]	116v–117r
69v	The Earles of Tholous [succ.]	117r
69v	The Earles of ffoix [succ.]	117r–v
70r–v	The Gouerment of Dolphine [top. desc.]	117v–118r
70v	The Dolphin of Vienois [succ.]	118v
70v–71r	The Prince of Orrenge [succ.]	118v
71r	The Dukes of Valentinois [succ.]	118v
71r–v	The Gouerment of Prouance [top. desc.]	118v–119v
71v–72r	The Earles of Prouance [succ.]	119v
	These two Duches vpon the Confines of Germanie and Ittalie, are now Accoumpted as members of the Crowne of France, but none of the xij Gouerments because thei be absolute Princes of themselues:	
72r	Loryane in Belgia [pol. desc.]	119v–120r
72r–73r	The Dukes of Lorayne [succ.]	120r–v
73r	The Duchie of Sauoye [top. desc.]	120v–121r
73v–74r	The Principalitie of Piemonte [top. desc.]	121r–v
74r–v	The Dukes of Savoye [succ.]	121v–122r
74v	What Weare and Marchandize are ordinarilie Carried out of France into our Partes and What they Retorne agayne	122v
91r–92r	[Index]	123r–v
76r–v	The Particular Succession and brefe Success of the French Kings	125r–130v
80r–84v, 89r–90v	[Coats of arms and notes on the chief families of France]	131r–134v

F1		F2
94r	Book III. Germanie	138r
94v	[Table of Contents]	138v
95r–v	The Generall Description of Germanie	139r–v
om.	[Geographical and political divisions of the provinces of "old Germany" and those which Germany has "gotten by Arms"]	140r
95v	The Cheifest Nauigable Riuers in Germanie	140r
95v–96v	The Gouerment of Germanie in generall	140v–142r
97r–v	The Pollicie of Germanie for the Administration of Iustice Generally	142r–143r
97v	The Pollicie of Germanie for the Administration of Iustice Particulerly, Vnder euerie Prince and Free States of the Empire	144r
98r	The particular Discriptions of Germanie According unto their Provincs and partes thereof	144r
98r	[Index to the provinces described below]	144r
98r–100v	The Suissers [hist., pol., and top. desc.]	144r–147r
100v–102v	The Suissers Commonwealth [pol. desc., administrative divisions, and military strength]	147r–149v
102v	ffriburge [succ.]	149v
102v	Kyburge [succ.]	149v
103r	Verdenberg [succ.]	149v
103r–104r	The Vpper Austria [top. desc.]	150r–151r
104r	Gortia and Tiroll [succ.]	151r
104r	Alsacia [succ.]	151r
104r–v	Montfort [succ.]	151v
104v	Phirreta [succ.]	151v
104v	Burgouia [succ.]	151v
105v	The Nether Austria [top. desc.]	151v–152v
105v	Austria [succ.]	152v–153r
105v	Carinthia [succ.]	153r

F1		F2
105r–106r	The manner in creating the Duke of Carinthia	153r–v
106r	Stiria [succ.]	153v
106r	Cillia [succ.]	153v
106v–107r	Bauaria [top. desc.]	153v–154v
107r	Bauarye [succ.]	154v–155r
107v	Landshutt [succ.]	155r
107v	Lewctenburg [succ.]	155r
107v	Wittelspach [succ.]	155r–v
107v	Ratisbon [succ.]	155v
107v	Crayburg [succ.]	155v
108r	Bogen or de la Arcu [succ.]	155v–156r
108r	Ottingen [succ.]	156r
108r–v	Sueuia [top. desc.]	156r–v
109r	Sweuia [succ.]	156v–157r
109r	Countie Pallatin of Rhine [succ.]	157r
109r	Wertinburg [succ.]	157r–v
109v	Teketh [succ.]	157v
109v	Badon [succ.]	157v–158r
109v	Hochburg [succ.]	158r
109v–110r	Zaringe [succ.]	158r
110r	Tubinge [succ.]	158r–v
110r	ffurstenburg [succ.]	158v
110r	Helphinstayn [succ.]	158v
110r–v	ffranconia [top. desc.]	158v–159r
110v–111r	The ffranconian Dukes [succ.]	159r–v
111r	The Installation of the Bishopp of Wirtzburge or Herbipolens	159v
111r–112r	Bohemia [top. desc.]	159v–160v
112r	Bohemia [succ.]	160v–161r
112v–113r	The Vpper Saxonie [top. desc.]	161r–162r
113r–v	The Dukes Electors of Saxonie [succ.]	162r–v
113v	Misina [succ.]	162v
113v	The Landgraues of Thuringe [succ.]	162v–163r
114r	Hasse [succ.]	163r
114r	Katsenelbogen [succ.]	163r
114r–v	The Nether Saxonie [top. desc.]	163r–164r
115r	The Count Pallatins of Saxonie [succ.]	164r–v

F1		F2
115r	The Dukes of Brunsuike from the Guelphes [succ.]	164v
115r	Luniburge [succ.]	165r
115v	Embeke [succ.]	165r
115v	Anhald and Lauenburge [succ.]	165r–v
115v	Holst [succ.]	165v
115v	Oldenburge [succ.]	165v
116r–v	Vandalia [top. desc.]	165v–166v
116v	Mekelburge [succ.]	166v
116v–117r	Pomerland [succ.]	166v–167r
117r	Brandeburg [succ.]	167r–v
117r	Prussia [succ.]	167v
117r–v	Nurenburg [succ.]	167v–168r
117v–118r	Westrich with all the west Coast of the Riuer of Rhine [top. desc.]	168r–169r
118r	Zewbrooke [succ.]	169r
118v	Iuliers [succ.]	169r
118v	Cleue [succ.]	169r–v
118v–119r	What ware and Merchaundize are ordinarily Carried out of Germanie into oure partes And what they retorne againe	169v
119r–v	The State of the Empire in Germanie as it is at this present vnder Rodulphus of Austria Emperour elect	169v–171r
120r–v	The first Institutions of the Tournaments in Germanie with certaine Articles concerninge the ordering thereof sett downe by Henry the first Emperour, and other Princes of Germanie	om.
121r	The Chiefe Peers of the Empire	om.
121v	The Marshallinge of the Princes and Potentatts of the Empire in the Emperiall Dietts	om.
123r	Certaine Kingdomes and Prouences borderinge vpon Germanie and doe almost inuiron the same:	171r

F1		F2
123r	A Shorte Discription of Hungarie, as it is vnder Rodulphus of Austria now king thereof, and Emperor Elect	171r–v
123r–v	The Regiment of Hungarie [succ.]	171v
123v–124v	The Kingdome of Poland [pol. and top. desc.]	172r–v
124v	The Gouerment of Polande	172v–173r
124v–125r	Denmarke [pol. and top. desc.]	173r–v
om.	The Gouerment of Denmark	173v
120v–121v	[Index]	174r–v
128r–v [frag.]	The Particular Succession and Brief Success of the Romane Emperors In Germany with ther Medialias to the Liffe	176r–179r
130r–141v	[Coats of arms and notes on the principal families of the Empire]	180r–183v
144r	Book IV. Belgia or the Netherlanders	187r
144v	[Table of Contents]	187v
145r	The Description of the Netherlanders, or the lowe Countries, in Generall	188r
145r	The Principall Riuers of these lowe Countries in Generall	188r
145r–146r	The Gouerment of these lowe Countries in general	188r–v
146r–v	The Pollicie for the Administration of Iustice particularlie in euery Prouence	189r
146v	Particuler Description of the Netherlanders according Vnto the Provinces and partes therof:	189r
146v	[Index to the counties described below]	189r
146v–147r	West ffrisland [top. desc.]	189v
147r–v	Gelderland, Zutphen and Ouerysell [top. desc.]	189v–190v

F1		F2
147v–148r	The Earles and Dukes of Guelders [succ.]	190v
148r–149r	Holland and Vtrich [top. desc.]	190v–191v
149r	Holland [succ.]	192r
149r–v	Zeland [top. desc.]	192r–v
149v–151r	Braband [top. desc.]	192v–194r
151r–v	The Dukes of Braband [succ.]	194v
151v–152r	Luxenburge [top. desc.]	194v–195r
152r	The Dukes of Luxemburg [succ.]	195v
152v	Namur [top. desc.]	195v–196r
152v	The Earles of Namur [succ.]	196r
153r–v	Haynault [top. desc.]	196r–197v
154r	The Erles of Haynault [succ.]	197v
154r–156v	ffllaunders [top. desc.]	197v–201v
156v–157r	The Earles of ffllaunders [succ.]	201v
157r	Artois [top. desc.]	202r
157v	The Earles of Artois [succ.]	202r–v
157v	Cambraye [succ.]	202v
157v–158r	Liege [top. desc.]	202v–203r
158r	Aix or Aken [top. desc.]	203r–v
158v	What Comodities is sent oute of these Lowe Countries Vnto other partes, and what they retorne againe	203v
158v	Certaine Decrees made by the Prince for the preseruation of the State [restrictions on trade in time of war, on trade with enemies, and on mercenary soldiers]	203v
158v	The 7 Principall Priuileges granted vnto the Brabanders by there owne Princes	203v
159v	The Counte Pallatine off Burgandie [hist. desc., top. desc., and succ.]	204r–v
159r–v	[Index]	205r–v
160r–161v	[Coats of arms and notes on the chief families of the Netherlands]	206r–209v
168r	Book V. Spaine	213r
168v	[Table of Contents]	213v

F1		F2
169r	The Generall Discription of Spain	214r–v
169v	The Principall Rivers of Spain	214v–215r
170r–v	The Goverment of Spaine in Generall	215r–v
170v–172r	The Pollicie of Spayne for the Administration of Iustice therein and for the Gouerment of that State in Generall	216r–217v
172r	Certaine causes alledged by the Ambassadors of France and Spaine before the Master of Ceremonies at Rome, in defence of their Masters Precedencye	om.
172v–173v	Gallicia [top. desc.]	218r–219v
174r	Galicia [succ.]	219v
174r	Leon [succ.]	219v
174r	Castella [succ.]	219v–220r
174r–v	Nauarr [succ.]	220r–v
175r	Biscaye [succ.]	220v
175r	ffrias [succ.]	220v–221r
175r	Medina del Rio Secco [succ.]	221r
175r	Naxara [succ.]	221r
175r	Pastrana [succ.]	221r
175v	Ariona [succ.]	221r
175v–176r	Tarracona [top. desc.]	221v–222v
176r–v	Arragon [succ.]	222v
176v–177r	Barcilona [succ.]	223r–v
177r	Segore and Cardona [succ.]	223v
177r	Trugill [succ.]	223v
177r–v	Carthagiena [top. desc.]	223v–224r
177v	Valentia [succ.]	224v
178r	Villa Hermosa [succ.]	224v
178r	Gandia and Lombay [succ.]	224v
178r–v	Betica [top. desc.]	224v–225v
178v	Cordoua [succ.: Kings of Cordova]	226r
179r	Ciuilia and Andaluzia [succ.: Kings of Seville and Andalusia]	226r–v
179r	Granada [succ.: Kings of Granada]	226v
179v	Medina Sidonia [succ.]	226v–227r
179v	Placentia and Bexare [succ.]	227r
179v	Arcos [succ.]	227r

F1		F2
179v	Ossunia [succ.]	227r
179v–180r	Sess [succ.]	227v
180r	Saffra [succ.]	227v
180r–181r	Lusitania [top. desc.]	227v–228r
181r–v	Portingall and Algraue [succ.]	228r–v
181v	Toledo and Valentia [hist. desc. of contention for the titles from 790 A.D. until the conquest by the Cid in 1088]	228v–229r
181v	Medina Cely [succ.]	229r
181v	Alua [succ.]	229r
181v–182r	Ascalonia [succ.]	229r–v
182r	Infantazgo [succ.]	229v
182r	Alberqueque [succ.]	229v
182r	Bragantia [succ.]	229v
182r	The Comodities of Spaine and Portingall which they sende into those partes, and what they retorne againe	230r
182v–183r	The Present State of Spayne	om.
om.	The deuision of the people in the Commonwealth of Spaine	230r–v
183r–v	[Index]	231r–v
184r–191v	The particular Succession and breffe Success of the Spanishe or Wisigothes in Spayn over the Principall kingdomes therof [also, the succ. of the Kings of Navarre, Aragon, and Portugal]	232r–238r
192r–193v	The Moores and Sarazen Kinges In Spaine	238v–240v
194r–198v	[Coats of arms and notes on the chief families in Spain]	241r–244r
199r–v	The late Musters of Spaine from 18 Vnto 50 Yeares of Age	om.
200r	The Parliament of the Estates of Spain	om.
203r	Book VI. England and Wales	248r
203v	[Table of Contents]	248v

F1		F2
204r–v	The generall Description of Englande	249–250r
205r–v	The Principall Nauigable and bounding Riuers of Englande and Wales	250r–251r
206r–207r	The Regiment of England In Generall	251r–252v
207r–208r	The Reuenues and proffittes, liable vnto the Crowne of England, aswell ordinary as extraordinarye with the Disbursments thereof	256r–v
208r–209v	The publique Lawes of Englande with the Pollicie therof for the Administracion of Iustice Ciuill and Criminall	252v–254v
210r–v	The particular gouerment of eche Province Seuerally for the Administracion of Iustice therin and well orderinge of the same	254v–255v
210v–211r	The publique gouerment of the State of Englande in generall	255v–256r
	The particular Description of England, accordinge vnto the vij Saxon Kingdomes erected therin subdeuided afterwardes Into xxxix prouances as followeth:	
211r	[Index to the Seven Saxon Kingdoms]	257r
211r–213r	The Kingdome of Kentt or by the Saxons called Centric contayning only the Countie of Kentt [top. desc. and hist. desc.]	257r–259v
213r–v	The Lord Wardens of the Cinque Portts [hist. of office, member towns and their charges]	259v–260r
213v–214r	[The Earls of Kent, succ.]	260r–v
214r–215r	The Southsaxon Kingdome [hist. and top. desc.]	260v
215v	[Sussex, top. desc.]	261r–262r
215r	[The Earls of Arundel]	262v
215v	Sussex [succ.]	262v
215v–216v	Surrey [top. desc.]	263r–264r
216v	Surrey [succ.]	264r

F1		F2
217r	The Kingdome of the East Angles [hist. and top. desc.]	264v
217r–v	Suffolk [top. desc.]	264v–265r
217v–218r	Suffolke [succ.]	265r–v
218r	Clare [succ.]	265v–266r
218r–v	Norffolke [top. desc.]	266r–267r
218v–219r	[Earls of Norfolk]	267r–v
219r–v	Cambridgshere [top. desc.]	267v–268r
219v	[The Earls of Cambridge]	268r–v
220r	The West Saxon Kingdome [hist. desc.]	268v–269r
220r–v	Cornwall [top. desc.]	269r–v
220v	Cornwall [succ.]	269v–270r
221r	The gouerment of the Stanery [pol. and admin. desc. of tin mines]	270r
221r–v	Deuonshere [top. desc.]	270r–271r
221v–222r	Deuonshere [succ.]	271r–v
222r	Dorcetshere [top. desc.]	271r–v
222v	[The Earls of Dorset]	271v
222v–223r	Somersetshere [top. desc.]	271v–273r
223r	[The Dukes and Earls of Somerset]	273r–v
223v	[The Earls of Bridgewater]	273v
223v	Bathe [succ.]	273v
223v–224r	Wiltshere [top. desc.]	273v–274v
224r	[The Earls of Wiltshire]	274v
224r–v	Salsburie [succ.]	275r
224v–225r	Hampshere [top. desc.]	275r–v
225r	Southampton [succ.]	276r
225r	Winchester [succ.]	276r
225r–v	Barkshere [top. desc.]	276v–277r
225v	[The Earls of Hungerford]	277r
226r	The kingdome of Northumberlande [hist. desc.]	277r–v
226r–227v	Yorkshire [top. desc.]	277r–279v
227v	Yorke [succ.]	279v–280r
228r	Holldernes [succ.]	280r
228r	Ritchmonde [succ.]	280r–v
228r–v	The Countie of Durham [top. desc.]	280v–281r
228v	[Counts Palatine of Durham, succ.]	281r
228v–229r	Lancashere [top. desc.]	281r–v

F1		F2
229r	[Dukes and Counts Palatine of Lancaster]	281v–282r
229v	Westmerland [top. desc.]	282r–v
229v	Westmerland [and the succ. of the Barons of Kendall]	282v
229v–230r	Cumberland [top. desc.]	283r
230r	[Earls of Cumberland]	283v
230r–v	Northumberland [top. desc.]	283v–284v
231r	[Dukes and Earls of Northumberland]	284v
231r	The East Saxon Kingdome [hist. desc.]	285r
231v–232r	The Countie of Middellsex [top. desc.]	285r–286v
232r–v	The Countie of Essex [top. desc.]	286v–287r
232v–233r	Essex [succ.]	287r–288r
233r–v	Hartfordshere [top. desc.]	288r–v
233v	[Earls of Hartford]	288v
233v	The Mercian Kingdome [hist. desc.]	288v–289r
233v–234r	Gloucestershere [top. desc.]	289r–v
234r–v	[Dukes and Earls of Gloucester]	290r–v
234v–235r	Oxfordshere [top. desc.]	290v–291v
235r	Oxforde [succ.]	291v
235v	Boukinghamshere [top. desc.]	291v–292r
235v	Boukingham [succ.]	292v
235v–236r	Bedfordshere [top. desc.]	292v–293r
236r	Bedforde [succ.]	293r
236v	Northampton [succ.]	294r
237r	Rivers [succ.]	294r–v
237r	Rutlandshere [top. desc.]	294v
237r	Rutlande [succ.]	294v–295r
237r–v	Lecestershere [top. desc.]	295r
237v	Hinklaye [succ.]	295v–296r
238r–v	Lincolnshere [top. desc.]	296r–297r
238v	[Dukes and Earls of Lincoln]	297r–v
238v	[Earls of Kyme]	297v
239r	Nottinghamshere [top. desc.]	297v–298r
239r	Nottingham [succ.]	298r
239v	Darbishere [top. desc.]	298r–v
239v–240r	Darbie [succ.]	298v–299r
240r–v	Warwickshere [top. desc.]	299r–v
240v	Warwicke [succ.]	299v–300r

F1		F2
241r	Arderne [succ.]	300r
241r–v	Worcestershere [top. desc.]	300r–301r
241v	Worcester [succ.]	301r
241v–242r	Staffordshere [top. desc.]	301r–v
242r	[Earls and Lords of Stafford]	301v–302r
242r–v	Shropshere [top. desc.]	302r–v
242v–243r	Shrewsbury [succ.]	302v–303r
243r–v	Cheshere [top. desc.]	303r–v
243v	Chester [succ.]	303v–304r
243v–244r	Huntingtonshere [top. desc.]	304r
244r	Huntington [succ.]	304r–v
244v–245r	The Discripton of all Walles in generall	305r–v
245–v	The particular Description and Regiment of Northwales	305v–306r
245v	Angliseye [top. desc.]	306v
245v–246r	Carnarvonshere [top. desc.]	306v–307r
246r	Merionetheshere [top. desc.]	307r
246r–v	Denbigheshere	307v
246v	[Lords of Denbighe]	307v
246v–247r	Flyntshere [top. desc.]	307v–308r
247r	Mongomerishere [top. desc.]	308r–v
247r	Powis [hist. desc. and succ. of kings]	308v
247v	The Description and Regiment of South Walles	309r
247v–248r	Carmarthenshire	309r–v
248r	Pembroke [top. desc.]	309v–310r
248r–v	Pembroke [succ.]	310r–v
248v–249r	Cardiganshire [top. desc.]	310v
249r	Glamorganshere [top. desc.]	310v–311r
249r	[Lords of Glamorgan]	311r
249v	Brechnockshere [top. desc.]	311v
249v	[Lords of Brechnock]	311v
249v–250r	Radnorshere [top. desc.]	311v–312r
250r	[Lords of Radnor]	312r
250r–v	Monmoutheshere [top. desc.]	312r–v
250v	Herifordshere [top. desc.]	312v–313r
250v–251r	Heryforde [succ.]	313r–v

F1		F2
251r–252r	The Diuision of the People in The English Common Wealthe Accordinge Vnto Ther seuerall Degrees therin off the Layetie	313v–314v
252r–v	The precedency of eche degree and officer, as thei were marshalled to attend the Queenes Maiestie in her goeing vnto Pooles in anno 1588 [Armada Victory Procession]	315r–v
253r–256r	The particular and breffe Success and succession of the Brittishe, Roman, Saxon, Danishe, and French Princes in the Regiment of England from Cesars time forward	316r–321r
256r–v	[Index]	321r–323v
258r–298v	[Coats of arms and notes on the chief families of England and Wales]	323r–339v
300r	Book VII. Scotlande	346r
om.	Table of Contents	346r
300v	[Index]	366r
300v	Principall Navigable and bounding Riuers	347r
301r–v	The general Descripcion of Scotlande	346r–347r
301v–303r	The Regiment of Scotland In generall from Cesars Time forward	347v–349r
303r–304r	The Lawes and Pollicies of Scotland for the Administracion of Iustice Ciuell and Criminall, With the gouerment of the State In generall and Perticularly	349r–350r
304r	The Reuenews Appertayning Vnto the Crowne of Scotland	350r
304v [frag.]	The South Partes of Scotland	350r–352v
om.	The Principall Clanes, and Surnames on the Borders	352v
	Gallawaye [succ.]	352v–353r
om.	Douglas [succ.]	353r
om.	Caryk [succ.]	353r

F1		F2
om.	Marche [succ.]	353r–v
om.	Bothwell [succ.]	353v
om.	Mourton [succ.]	353v
om.	Eglington [succ.]	353v
om.	Cassell [succ.]	353v–354r
307r–v	The West partes of Scotlande [top. desc.]	354r–v
307v	Argile [succ.]	354v
307v–308r	Lenox [succ.]	355r
308r	Arran [succ.]	355r
	Glencar [succ.]	355r
308r–v	The North Partes of Scotland [top. desc.]	355r–356r
308v	Rosse [succ.]	356r
om.	Huntley [succ.]	356r
om.	Southerland [succ.]	356r
om.	Cathnes [succ.]	356v
om.	Orkney [succ.]	356v
311r–v [frag.]	The Easte Partes of Scotlande [top. desc.]	356v–358v
311v	ffiffe [succ.]	358v
312r	Angushe [succ.]	358v
312r	Murrey [succ.]	359r
312r	Arroll [succ.]	359r
312v	Crawforde [succ.]	359r
312v	The Earle Marshall [succ.]	359v
312v	Bouchquhan [succ.]	359v
312v	Rothesay [succ.]	359v
312v	Marr [succ.]	359v
312v	Montrose [succ.]	359v
313r	Gorrey [succ.]	360r
313r	Mentithe [succ.]	360r
313r	[List of the counties assigned to the four quarters of Scotland]	360r
316v	[Term and schedule of the "Sessions Table" at Edinburgh]	360r
316v	The Diuision of the People in the Scottishe Commonwealthe, accordinge to ther seuerall Degrees	360v

F1		F2
313r–316r	The particular Succession and brefe Success of the Scottishe Kinges seated in greate Brittaine from Caesars Time forwarde	361r–365v
317r–328v	[Coats of arms and notes on the chief families of Scotland]	378r–383r
333r	The Navie Royall of England [list of ships, their weight, number of guns and sailors necessary to man them]	om.
333v	[List of English ordnance commonly in use]	om.
334r–v	Ordinary charges of the English Crown	om.
337r	Book VIII. Irlande	386r
339r–v	The Political Description of Irland generally	387r–v
339v–340r	The Successiue Regiment of Irlande In generall	387v–388v
340r–v	The Pollicie of Irland for the Administracion of Iustice	388v
	The Geographicall Description of Irland particularly according vnto the 5 principall kingdomes or Regions therof:	
340v–341r	Munster [top. desc.]	389r–v
341r	Desmonde [succ.]	389v
341v	Glencar [succ.]	389v
341v–342r	Lenster and Meth [top. desc.]	389v–390v
342r	Leynster [succ.]	390v–391r
342r	Kildare [succ.]	391r
342v	Ormond [succ.]	391r
342v	Meth [succ.]	391r
342v	Conagh [top. desc.]	391r–v
342v–343r	Conagh [succ.]	391v
343r	Thomond [succ.]	391v
343r–v	Vulster [top. desc.]	391v–392v
343v–344r	The Ile off Wight [top. desc.]	392v
344r	Ierosey [top. desc.]	392v

F1		F2
344r	Garnsey [top. desc.]	392v–393r
344r–v	The Ile off Man [top. desc.]	393r
345r–348v	[Coats of arms and notes on the chief families of Ireland]	394r–395v

[Turkish Empire]

349r–v	[Fragment of a chronology of Sultans, 1300–1595]	om.
349v [frag.]	[Description of the Turkish Government]	om.

Appendices
Dedication (F2)
Perigrinationis Ratio (F2)

[iii^r] To the Highe and: Mightie Prince, my most gratius Soueraigne/ Ieames by the grace off God King off England, Scotland, France, and Ireland, Defendor of the Faith etc./ Edmund Tyllney Master off your Maiesties Reuells, Wisheth long lieffe, and perfitt health, With a longe and Prosperus Raigne ouer vs:

Although Right Highe and Mightie Prince, that many great learned Men, haue much traueled: in the Discriptions off Contries/ Somm perticularlie off one Cuntrie/ and somme off another/ som of one matter therin, and somme off another/ and somme generallie off all Cuntries alike/ / yet hath ther not hitherto comm vnto my handes, any one of them, Which hath either so particularly, or generally, proceeded therein, that the Estate off any one of thos Cuntries, coulde be Well conceiued, otherwise then Geographecally/ / Neither do I heareby presume to presentt the same, being a Matter off so great Difficultie/ / But because many years sens, When I first became to be a Courtior, and had then begun after some sortt, to trauell therein, In sofarforth as vnto an Intertaininge Courtior appertained, and for my own priuatt

Satesfaction, to Collecte, and gather certaine speciall Notes generally, Concerninge the same/ groundinge myselfe only, for the more Certainty therein, vppon the home-borne Writters (for Matters by paste) Written off ther own naturall Cuntries/ / In Whom notwithstanding, I founde such vncertainties, and Contrarieties, that I grew almost Wearie theroff/ yet still, vrged thervnto, by the earnest desier I had, sumwaies to satisffie my selfe att the least therin, althoughe not as I Would, yett as I could/ and thervppon, I traualed so much as appertained vnto me to Reconsile thos Aucthors, by Comparing certaine generallities, With ther particulars theroff/ obseruing only that to my selfe, Which in my own Concepte, Carried greatest reason, and likelihood off troth/ / So for the presentt state off thinges, I haue vsed the like best Courss, by my own trauaill, and by Relation off suche, as had best Meanes to know the trueth/ / Referring notwithstanding, the Refformation—aswell off the one, as of the other, vnto any Person off greater Experiens, and sounder Iudgmentt/ / (ffor all Men ar Commonlie partiall, in ther own labors) So when I had spente many yeares, In this most Intricated laborinth, and found thos Collections off myne, to rise vnto a farr greater Vollume then I Expected (although to little for so many Matters) I thought it then no Charritie, Wholy to Conceale the same/ And thervppon, first began to Deuide thos Indigested labours off myne, into some forme, and to Marshall thos Cuntries Which I hadd most trauailed in, Into one Vniforme Methode through them all/ by deuiding them, into viij speciall Bookes, According vnto the viij seuerall Cuntries chiffly Described therby/ beginninge eache Booke, with the generall Discription and gouermentt off that Cuntrie generally/ and by Subdeuidinge off the same, Into Prouinces, or Shires, as Well the Particulare gouerment thereof, as also the Principall Citties, and Townes for trade or strenkth, With the cheiffe Possessioners, and

Inhabitors off the same ar breiflie sett downe/ / Concludinge eache booke, With a Cronologie of the Perticular Succession, and breife Success off all suche Emprors, and Kinges, as haue Absolutelie Comaunded, and gouerned the same, togeather With certaine off the most Antientest Famelies theroff, and ther Armes so farr forth as came vnto Knowledg/ / All Which Cuntries beinge thus Marshalled, yett thought I them not fitt, for certaine Respectes, to be Published vnto the Common Vew, and Censure of the ignorantt/ but rather to presente the same, vnto some person of Worth, that In his own greate Experience, and graue Iudgmentt, might beste, and Iustly, allowe or Condemne the same/ / And which att this Presentt, Right Highe, and Mightie Prince, most happely falleth out, Iff that itt Would please your most Royall Maiestie, to vouchsaffe the exceptans of so simple a Presentt, Prostrated by your most loyall Seruantt, att your Maiesties ffeete/ / Not as any Matter therin Contained, vnknowen vnto your Maiestie alreadie, but as a breuiate vnto your Highnes Memorie, for matters of chiffest Note therin, vppon any suddaine, not hauing the leysore for euerie cause, to ouerturne so many great Vollumes/ / The gratious Acceptans Whereoff, Will add many yeares more, vnto the olde age off your Maiesties most deuoted Seruantt/ / and further bound therby (iff itt maie be), dailie to praie for your Maiesties most long, and Prosperus Raigne ouer vs:/ /

Your Maiesties most loyall Subiect
and ffaithfull Seruante

Edmond Tyllney:/

[ii^{r}] The Topographicall descriptions Regimentes and Pollicies off Ittalie, France, Germanie: England, Spayne, Scotland and Ireland Wherby In somm sorte the Particulare Estates off euerie one off thos Contries maie be Discouered:

For the better conceuing the Estate off any one of thes Cuntries obserue Well hearby

- The Description off the Contrie
  - Whether it be greate or small and how Peopled:
  - Whether itt be ffructfull or Barren with the chifest Home Commodities thereof:
  - Whether it be Well fortified or not and how mainteined.
  - And how itt lieth Scittuated for Inuasion or Reliffe.
- The Worth off the People
  - Whether thei be Warlike or basse mynded: and how trayned:
  - Whether thei be loyall vnto ther Prince or Seditious and how gouerned:
  - Whether thei be Wealthie or Beggerlie—and what be ther chiffe trades:/
  - And Whether thei be Vnited or deuided by Factions:
- And the Abillitie off the Prince
  - Whether he be Martiallie mineded: or A Pollitician:
  - How his Coffers be filled: with Coyne and What meanes to Increase the same:
  - How: Allied with Kindred and Freindes and what Intelligence With his Neighbors:
  - And how he standeth affected In Matters of Religion:/

PERIGRINATIONIS RATIO

NOTES

I. EDMOND TYLLNEY

1. When he testified in a Chancery suit on 10 August 1599 (P.R.O. C24/272/44) Tyllney gave his age as 63. For a more detailed discussion of the documents on which his biography is based see W. R. Streitberger, "On Edmond Tyllney's Biography," *Review of English Studies,* n.s. 29 (1978), 11–35.

2. Pishey Thompson, *The History and Antiquities of Boston* (London: Longmans, 1856), pp. 373–74.

3. From an inscription on his funeral monument at St. Leonard's Church, Streatham. A photograph (R. C. H. M. BB76/4925) is held by the National Archives; the inscription is printed by Manning and Bray, III, p. 391.

4. *Letters and Papers, Foreign and Domestic, of the Reign of Henry VIII,* ed. R. H. Brodie (London: Longman & Co., 1920), XVI, pp. 684–85; see also pp. 608–9, 618, 635, 680, and XVII, pp. 13–62.

5. F. B. Benger, "Edmund Tilney, A Leatherhead Worthy," *Proceedings of the Leatherhead and District L. H. S.,* 1 (1950), 16.

6. See Robert W. Kenny, *Elizabeth's Admiral* (Baltimore, Md.: Johns Hopkins University Press, 1970).

7. Granville Leveson-Gower, "The Howards of Effingham," *Surrey Archaeological Collections,* 9 (1888), 425.

8. Manning and Bray, II, p. 233; Eccles, *Buc,* p. 425.

9. John Stow, *Chronicles* (London, 1615), p. 675.

10. E. K. Chambers, "The Elizabethan Lords Chamberlain," Malone Society Reprints, *Collections,* I (1911), 31–32; and *The Elizabethan Stage,* (Oxford: Clarendon Press, 1923), I, 39.

11. S. T. C. 24076–24077a.5. There may have been six editions: two in 1568, one in 1571, one in 1573, one in 1577, and one again in 1587. On the possibility of two 1568 editions, see J. G. Tilney-Basset, "Edmund Tilney's *The Flower of Friendshippe,*" *The Library,* Fourth Series, 26 (1945), 175–81.

12. F. S. Boas, "Queen Elizabeth, the Revels Office and Edmund Tilney," in *Queen Elizabeth in Drama and Related Studies* (London: Allen and Unwin, 1950), p. 47.

13. C. S. Lewis, *English Literature in the Sixteenth Century Excluding Drama* (Oxford: Clarendon Press, 1954), p. 246.

14. Baldassare Castiglione, *The Courtyer,* tr. T. Hoby (London, 1561); G. Boccaccio, *A pleasaunt disport of diuers noble personages entitled Philocopo,* tr. G[ranthum] (London, 1566); Pedro de Lujan, *Coloquios Matrimoniales* (Sevill, 1550); and see E. J. Moncada, "The Spanish Source of Edmund Tilney's 'The Flower of Friendshippe'," *Modern Language Review,* 65 (1970), 241–47.

15. Feuillerat, *Documents,* pp. 256, 270; Chambers, *Elizabethan Stage,* II, 134–35; IV, 151–53.

16. Printed in Feuillerat, *Documents,* p. 55; he was preferred to the post by his cousin, Lord Charles Howard (P.R.O. C2 Jas. I. E6/29).

17. Feuillerat, *Documents,* pp. 5–17, 411, 474; Chambers *Elizabethan Stage,* I, 82–84.

18. Feuillerat, *Documents,* p. 206.

19. Feuillerat, *Documents,* p. 359; Chambers, *Elizabethan Stage,* II, 104–15.

20. Sydney Anglo, *Spectacle, Pageantry, and Early Tudor Policy* (Oxford: Clarendon Press, 1968), pp. 117–18.

21. Feuillerat, *Documents,* pp. 193, 220, 320–21, 332.

22. F. S. Boas, *op. cit.,* p. 49; Feuillerat, *Documents,* pp. 51–52, prints the commission.

23. Chambers, *Elizabethan Stage,* IV, 319–30; *Henslowe's Diary,* ed. W. W. Greg, 2 vols. (London: A. H. Bullen 1904–08), I, 130–60.

24. In a letter from Walsingham to Burghley on 6 August 1581: Sir Dudley Digges, *The Compleat Ambassador* (London, 1655), p. 359.

25. W. R. Streitberger, "The Armada Victory Procession and Tudor Precedence," *Notes & Queries,* 225 (1980), 310–12.

26. Feuillerat, *Documents,* p. 50.

27. J. L. Chester, *Allegations for Marriage Licenses Issued by the Bishop of London, 1520–1610,* ed. G. T. Armytage, *Harleian Society,* 25 (London, 1887), I, p. 118.

28. P.R.O. Prob. 11/63, f. 22.

29. Manning and Bray, I, p. 518.

30. P.R.O. A03/128, 1590–91; Chambers, *Elizabethan Stage,* IV, 106.

31. A. R. Bax, "The Lay Subsidy Assessments for the County of Surrey," *Surrey Archaeological Collections,* 18 (1903), 200, 210.

32. J. C. Jeaffreson, "The MSS. of W. M. Molyneux, Esq." *7th Report, R. C. H. M.* (London, 1879), p. 662; W. R. Streitberger, "A Letter from Edmond Tyllney to Sir William More," *Surrey Archaeological Collections,* 71 (1977), 225–31; and F. B. Benger, *op. cit.,* p. 10.

33. For a more detailed account of these suits see W. R. Streitberger, "On Edmond Tyllney's Biography," *Review of English Studies,* n.s. 29 (1978), 11–35.

34. *C. S. P. Dom.,* II, p. 354; *Cobbett's Complete Collection of State Trials,* ed. T. B. Howell (London, 1809), pp. 1141–60.

35. P.R.O. Star Ch. T31/37.

36. P.R.O. C2/ Jas. I. E6/29.

37. *Gesta Grayorum,* ed. W. W. Greg. Malone Society Reprints (Oxford, 1914); J. Nichols, *The Progresses and Public Processions of Queen Elizabeth* (London, 1788), II; (London, 1823), II, p. 262.

38. Chambers, *Elizabethan Stage,* I, 91–93.

39. The letters are printed in *The Complete Works of John Lyly,* ed. R. W. Bond, 3 vols. (Oxford: Clarendon Press, 1902), I, 64, 68, 70, 378, 392, 395; see the corrections and discussion in Eccles, *Buc,* pp. 431–34.

40. P.R.O. E403/2561, 1603–11, f. 4; cf. Chambers, *Elizabethan Stage,* I, 53n; III, 377.

41. P.R.O. E351/2805, 1603–10; A01/2046, rolls 10–17.

42. The date of his death is given in a statement by Herbert in a declaration on 6 May 1662; J. Q. Adams, *The Dramatic Records of Sir Henry Herbert* (Ithaca, N.Y.: Cornell University Press, 1917), p. 108.

43. The will (Prob. 11/116s [register book copy] and Prob. 10/270/Oct. 1610 [office copy] was probated on 17 October 1610; a summary is given by Boas, *op. cit.,* pp. 52–55. Strea-

tham Parish Register, P95–LEN, Greater London Record Office, records his burial on 6 October 1610.

II. TOPOGRAPHICAL DESCRIPTIONS

1. *Profitable Instructions: Describing what Speciall obseruations are to be taken by Trauellers in all Nations, States and Countries,* ed. B[enjamin] F[isher] (London, 1633), p. 24. Attributed to William Davidson, Principal Secretary (30 Sept. 1586–ca. 1590).
2. Aristotle, *Politics,* IV, 1289b, ff.
3. See Chapter VII.

III. HISTORICAL AND LITERARY SIGNIFICANCE OF THE WORK

1. Jerome Turler, *The Traveiler,* intro. D. E. Baughan (1575; rpt. Gainesville, Fla.: Scholar Facsimile, 1951), sig. Aiiij^{r}. See also G. C. Moore Smith, *Gabriel Harvey's Marginalia* (Stratford-upon-Avon: Shakespeare Head Press, 1913).
2. *Profitable Instructions: Describing what Speciall obseruations are to be taken by Trauellers in all Nations, States and Countries,* ed. B[enjamin] F[isher] (London, 1633), sigs. A1^{r}–A3^{r}.
3. In his letter to the Earl of Rutland, (*Profitable Instructions,* pp. 27–28) Essex states, "I hold it for a principle in the course of Intelligence of State, not to discourage men of meane capacity from writing vnto me; though I had at that same time very able aduertisements: for either they sent mee matter which the other omitted, or made it clearer." J. Spedding, *The Letters and the Life of Francis Bacon,* 7 vols. (London: Longmans, 1861), II, 6–15, collates this letter with other witnesses and argues that it was written by Bacon.
4. Turler, p. 50; cf. *R.S.V.* Numbers, 13:1–24.
5. Turler, sig. Aiii^{v}; see Clare M. Howard, *English Travelers of the Renaissance* (London: John Lane, 1914), pp. 205–23, and Edward G. Cox, *A Reference Guide to the Literature of Travel,* 3 vols. (Seattle: University of Washington Press, 1935, 1938, 1949), II, 320. Cox lists two books published before Turler's.
6. Albert Meier, *Certain briefe and special Instructions for Gentlemen, merchants, students, souldiers, marriners, &c. Employed in seruices abrode, or in anie way occasioned to conuerse in the*

kingdomes, and gouernementes of ffore Princes, tr. Philip Jones (London, 1589), sig. A3r.

7. *Profitable Instructions,* p. 76.

8. Sloane MS. 1813 (quoted by Howard, p. 40).

9. *C. S. P. Dom.,* vol. lxxvii, no. 6.

10. Meier, sig. A2r.

11. *Profitable Instructions,* pp. 2–24; Howard, p. 36, suggests the date 1595. I have modernized the spelling and somewhat altered the form, although not the arrangement, of the material.

12. Turler, p. 59.

13. Francis Peck printed from some of these manuscripts in *Desiderata Curiosa* (London, 1732), I, bk. ii. I have seen one at the University of Illinois, ca. 1579, several at the Folger and at the Huntington. Folger MS. V.b. 113 (ca. 1595), with the exception of the appendix on Spain, is typical of these documents.

14. Folger MS. V.b. 113 (ca. 1595).

15. *Profitable Instructions,* pp. 78–79.

16. See T. D. Kendrick, *British Antiquity* (London: Methuen, 1950).

17. Harrison, *Description of Britain,* bk. ii, ch. 16, gives the figure as 1,172,674, but the tables of musters printed by Francis Peck in *Desiderata Curiosa,* 2 vols. (London, 1732), I, bk. ii, 22–23, indicate that the total was 182,929, which agrees with "A Brefe Summarie and Demonstracion of the Estate of England and Wales" (ca. 1579), University of Illinois MS., uncat., ff. 13r–14r.

18. See below under Sources.

19. *The Profession of Dramatist in Shakespeare's Time* (Princeton, N.J.: Princeton University Press, 1971), pp. 146–96.

20. Chambers, *Elizabethan Stage,* IV, 305–06.

21. Harleian MS. 7368; see A. W. Pollard et al., *Shakespeare's Hand in the Play of Sir Thomas More* (1923; rpt. Cambridge University Press, 1967); and R. W. Chambers, *Man's Unconquerable Mind* (London: Jonathan Cape, 1939), ch. 6.

22. R. C. Bald, "The Book of Sir Thomas More and Its Problems," *Shakespeare Survey,* 2 (1949), 50.

23. T. W. Baldwin, *On the Literary Genetics of Shakespeare's Plays* (Urbana: University of Illinois Press, 1959), p. 465n.

24. Chambers, *Elizabethan Stage,* IV, 306–07.

25. The editors of the Oxford Shakespeare intend to restore the original name.

IV. SOURCES AND INFLUENCES

1. "Notes on the Present State of Christendome," (ca. 1582): J. Spedding, *op. cit.*, I, 18–30.
2. *The Description of the Low Countries and of the Provinces thereof*, tr. Thomas Dannet (London, 1593).
3. Guicciardini, p. 172; Dannet, f. 58^{v}.
4. Mexia's work, enlarged in Italian by Lodovico Dulce and Girolamo Bardi, was translated by W. T[raheron] (London, 1604).
5. Sir Robert Dallington, The View of France [1604], published by the Shakespeare Association in 1936.
6. From an edition later than 1579 of Abraham Ortelius, *Theatrum Orbis Terrarum.*
7. Folger MS. V.b. 113 (ca. 1595).
8. Raphael Mafei, *Commentariorum Vrbanorum* (Basil, 1530).
9. Polydore Vergil, *Anglicae Historia* (Basil, 1555); Elias Reusner, *op. cit.;* Claudius Ptolemy, *Geography* (Bononie, 1462): many subsequent editions and translations; *The Eight Books of Julius Caesar,* tr. A. Golding (London, 1590); Lodovico Guicciardini, *op. cit.*
10. Raphael Holinshed et al., *Chronicles* (London, 1587); William Harrison, *Description of Britain,* in Holinshed; John Stow, *The Annales of England* (London, 1592); Giraldus, "Itinerarium Cambriae," "Cambriae Descriptio" in *Britannicae Historia Libri Sex,* ed. Ludovicus Verunnius Ponticus (London, 1585), pp. 47–230; 231–77; Ralphe Brooke, *A Discoverie of certain errors published in . . . Britannia* (London, 1594); Caradoc of Llancarvan, *The History of Cambria,* tr. H. Lhuyd, ed. D. Powel (London, 1584).
11. See Description of the Manuscripts, below.
12. Maitland's introduction to Sir Thomas Smith, *De Republica Anglorum,* ed. L. Alston (Cambridge: The University Press, 1906), pp. xvi–xxi; see Harrison, *Description,* bk. ii, ch. 8 and Smith, *De Republica,* bk. ii, chs. 1–2.
13. See above, section II, n. 13.
14. Tyllney's description of this procession is more complete than either Harleian MS. 894, f. 3a–b (cf. chapter I, n. 25,

above) or the accounts in Nichols, *Progresses and Public Processions* (1788), II, 64–69; (1823), II, 537–44. For a description of the procession see Stow, *Annales* (1605), pp. 1260–61; Camden, *Annales of Elizabeth,* tr. R. N[orton], 3rd ed. (London, 1635), p. 144; and, for another manuscript chart of the procession, Folger MS. V.a. 213 (ca. 1605), pp. 55–58.

15. *The Itinerary of John Leland,* ed. Lucy Toulmin Smith, 5 vols. (London: G. Bell and Sons, 1907–10.

16. From the dedication to Sir William Brooke, Lord Cobham, in Holinshed et al., *op. cit.*

17. T. D. Kendrick, *British Antiquity* (London: Methuen, 1950), p. 139.

18. First published in 1586, *Britannia* went through six increasingly larger Latin editions in the author's lifetime; there were also Continental editions and an English version printed in England in 1610; see F. J. Levy, "The Making of Camden's Britannia," *Bibliothèque d'Humanisme et Renaissance,* 26 (1964), 70–97.

19. Francis Bacon, *Historie of the Rayne of King Henry the Seventh* (London, 1622), p. 18.

V. REVISIONS

1. See Edmond Tyllney, above.

2. *Complete Peerage,* XII, pt. 2, 128–29.

3. In order, these documents are Loseley MSS., vol. II, #98; B. L., Lansdowne MS., 83, f. 170; B. L. Harleian MS. 7368; Folger MS. V.b. 182; University of Illinois MS., uncat.; P.R.O. A03/907, 1585 (duplicate); the signatures are on the Revels Office Books, Pipe Office and Audit Office Accounts from 1578 until 1609. On Tyllney's contributions to F2, see W. R. Streitberger, "Some New Specimens of Edmond Tyllney's Hand," *The Library,* Sixth Series 28 (1975), 151–55.

VI. PROVENANCE

1. Sir G. F. Warner and J. P. Gilson, *Catalogue of the Western Manuscripts in the Old Royal and King's Collections* (London, 1921), I, p. xi.

2. Michael Rabbett, Rector of Streatham, Surrey, 1585–1630, d. 5 February 1630: *Alumni Cantabrigienses,* ed. J. Venn and J. A. Venn (Cambridge: Cambridge University Press, 1922–27), pt. 1, III, p. 413; *R. C. H. M., Salisbury* (Cecil), XVII, p. 406; P.R.O. Prob. 11/159. c/2018. Griffith Vaughan, Rector of Ashted, Surrey, 1587–1612: *Alumni Oxonienses, 1500–1714,* ed. Joseph Foster (Oxford: Clarendon Press, 1891), IV, p. 1553; P.R.O. Prob. 11/121. c/2018.

3. Buc is praised by Camden in *Britannia* (1600), p. 726, for supplying him with information, and by Edmond Howes, editor of Stowe's *Annales* (1615), sig. Oooo4^{v}, for the contribution of his essay "The Third University of England." He also wrote a *History of Richard III* and the lost "Art of the Revels."

4. See Eccles, *Buc,* p. 494.

5. While Selden died on 30 November 1654, it was not until 1659 that his executors sent his library of some 8,000 volumes to the Bodleian; meanwhile, many of the volumes were borrowed or lost. See W. D. Macray, *Annals of the Bodleian Library* (Oxford: Clarendon Press, 1890), 2nd ed., pp. 110–23.

6. F2, f. 334^{v}.

7. *Complete Peerage,* III, p. 92 ff.

8. De Ricci, 1300.1.

9. *Dictionary of National Biography* and *Corrections and Additions to the D. N. B.* (Boston: G. K. Hall, 1966), p. 208.

10. Folger MSS., MA 243, MA 279, Mb 58, Wb 258, and Wb 259; MA 280 and 281 were sent in November 1924.

11. On the Foley family see T. R. Nash, *Collections for the History of Worcestershire* (London, 1799), 2nd ed., II, pp. 460–62, App., pp. 82–84; and H. Sydney Grazebrook, *The Heraldry of Worcestershire* (London: J. R. Smith, 1873), Pt. I, p. 27.

12. Catalogues of the Foley library which have survived are scattered throughout England and the United States: *Robert Foley, Dean of Worcester,* R. Faulder, 1786 (British Library); *Thomas Foley, Baron of Kidderminster,* T. King, 18 March 1795 (Bodleian Library); *Lord Foley of Witley Court,* 1813 (Grolier Club Library, New York); *Adrian Gerald, 8th Baron Foley,* Anderson #1607, 30 November 1921 (American Antiquarian Society Library); F2 appeared for sale in the *Catalogue of the Library of the Right Honorable Lord Foley* [Henry Gerald, 7th Baron Foley], Ruxley Lodge, Claygate, Surrey, Castiglione and

Scott, 23, 24, 25 October 1919, p. 8, item #67 (J. P. R. Lyell's annotated copy is now in the Newberry Library, Chicago).

VII. DESCRIPTION OF THE MANUSCRIPTS

1. A preliminary description of F1 appeared in my "The Tyllney Manuscript at the Folger Library," *Publications of the Bibliographical Society of America,* 69 (1975), 449–64.

2. For the distribution of the artists' work in F2 see my "Edmond Tyllney's Topographical Descriptions, Regiments, and Policies of England and Wales," *Diss.* University of Illinois, 1973, pp. 30–33.

Index